A-Z *of*
SPECIAL NEEDS

- **A–Z of conditions**
  - **Who's who**
  - **Resources**
  - **Jargon-buster**

Jacquie Buttriss and Ann Callander

pfp
teacherbooks

© pfp publishing limited 2003

First published in Britain in 2003 by
pfp publishing limited
61 Gray's Inn Road
London WC1X 8TH

Editors and writers Jacquie Buttriss and Ann Callander
Cover design PinkFrog
Page design Linda Reed and Associates

Printed and bound in the UK by Ashford Colour Press Ltd, Gosport, Hampshire.

Reprinted 2003

A catalogue record for this book is available from the British Library.

ISBN 1 874050 77 5

pfp orders and customer services
FREEPOST LON20579
London WC1X 8BR

Tel: 0845 602 4337   Fax: 0845 602 4338
www.pfp-publishing.com

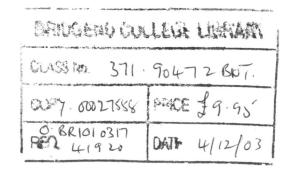

Contents

Introduction

This book provides a definitive A–Z reference for teachers who work with special needs children and for busy special needs coordinators, who often know a great deal about many issues and the general range of learning difficulties children have, but need a quick and easy look-up guide. This A–Z is intended to help you to answer specific questions such as

- where can I find appropriate learning resources for a child with …?

- who publishes books about special needs conditions, such as …?

- which support group can help the parents of a child with …?

- which specialist can I consult about the specific needs of a child with …?

- how can I explain to parents the special needs jargon in an assessment report?

- what exactly is a 'note in lieu'?

- what are the characteristics and implications of a new child's syndrome and is there a website for it?

This book is by no means a complete answer to everything (well, not quite), but it is designed to provide every teacher and special needs coordinator with a comprehensive reference resource. All contact details provided are correct at time of going to press.

Barriers to learning

A–Z of special needs conditions, syndromes and learning difficulties.

The 2001 SEN Code of Practice uses the term 'barriers to learning' to include all types of special needs conditions, syndromes and learning difficulties. This section provides a description of the main barriers to learning, including any medical symptoms and identified variations, which may affect a child's access to the curriculum. Key characteristics are listed, especially those relating to learning. For each condition, syndrome or learning difficulty, we recommend a range of useful support strategies. Contact details for the support agencies named can be found in the A–Z of special needs support groups on pages 49–56.

Advice should always be sought from the appropriate specialists, who will often be able to give you more detailed recommendations or support programmes for any individual child.

It is important to remember that every named condition, syndrome or learning difficulty will cover a spectrum and that the descriptions given here are for typical cases. The sorts of characteristics that children with these barriers to learning might demonstrate to a greater or lesser degree are outlined. Some children will exhibit nearly all the key characteristics, while others will have very few.

Barriers to learning contents

Aphasia

Aphasia is the inability to express thoughts in words, or the inability to understand thoughts expressed in the spoken or written words of others. Aphasia can range from mild to severe.

- **Global aphasia** is the severest form, where the child has either very little understanding of or very little ability to use spoken language.
- **Broca's aphasia** (non-fluent aphasia) results in the understanding but limited use of vocabulary and slow, laborious speech.

Other types of aphasia have also been identified.

Aphasia in children is quite rare and is usually the result of damage to the brain through birth trauma, stroke, brain tumour, infection or accident. It is usually treated through speech and language therapy. Aphasia affects one or more of a person's language functions, depending on the part of the brain that has been damaged.

Key characteristics

Children with aphasia may

- have expressive language difficulties, but an understanding of some spoken language
- sometimes have difficulty swallowing

- have receptive language difficulties (trouble understanding meaning), but be able to speak using a limited vocabulary
- have difficulties learning to read and write.

Support strategies

All support strategies should be implemented under the guidance of a speech and language therapist. They may include

- exercises for the facial muscles
- speech-sound activities
- noun picture cards to improve memory of object names
- learning sign language
- using ICT to support development of speech, hearing and reading comprehension.

Support agencies

- British Institute for Brain Injured Children (BIBIC)
- Cerebra

Apraxia

Developmental verbal apraxia is the inability to coordinate the lip, tongue and throat muscles in order to form sounds into words. No two children with apraxia are alike in the characteristics they display. Children with developmental verbal apraxia may coordinate other movements normally.

Key characteristics

Children with developmental verbal apraxia may

- be able to move the muscles used for speech but be unable to make words
- understand what others are saying but have difficulty replying
- have difficulty imitating speech
- be able to say short words but have difficulty with longer words and sentences
- be able to say a word correctly once, but then be unable to repeat it
- have other coordination difficulties
- have other language difficulties
- have attention difficulties

- have difficulties with self-monitoring of speech production
- have some behavioural difficulties.

Support strategies

All support strategies should be implemented under the guidance of a speech and language therapist. Therapy may include

- speech-sound activities
- exercises to improve planning, sequencing and coordination of motor movements for speech production
- using rhythm and music to help develop sound combinations
- modelling motor movements used to produce specific sounds and words
- encouraging self-monitoring of speech production.

Support agencies

- Speech Teach

Arthritis

There are three main types of juvenile arthritis.

- **Pauci-articular juvenile arthritis** usually starts very slowly, at age two or three, and symptoms are limited to four or fewer joints (usually the large joints such as knees, ankles or elbows) which become inflamed and painful. The child's eyes can also be affected by a condition known as iridocyclitis, which is inflammation in the front of the eye.

- **Poly-articular juvenile arthritis** affects five or more joints (often in the hands or feet) and can start at any age. It usually spreads from one joint to another quite quickly. Children with this type of arthritis may often feel unwell and suffer from a fever or a rash.

- **Systemic juvenile arthritis** affects the whole body and causes fevers and rashes as well as swollen joints. It can also affect the internal organs. Systemic disease usually starts in pre-school children and is also known as Stills disease.

Arthritis in children is usually referred to as juvenile idiopathic arthritis, although it used to be known as juvenile chronic arthritis. About one in a thousand children has arthritis. Some will be more severely affected than others and most will have periods of remission, when symptoms will be mild, interspersed with more acute periods. In some children, it can change from day to day. Periods when the arthritis is particularly active are called flares.

Juvenile arthritis is not contagious and is thought to be an auto-immune disease. Falls and sudden changes in temperature can aggravate the condition and, in some cases, it is important to try to avoid contact with some childhood illnesses, especially chickenpox.

During a flare, the child will probably be reluctant to use the joints, limping or showing reluctance to walk for example, or to use both hands for a task. Stiffness is also a feature. When a joint is inflamed, the child will probably be most comfortable if the joint is rested in a bent position, but it will need to be straightened from time to time to prevent damage. Some children will eventually outgrow their arthritis, but others will develop joint damage and can have difficulties, often getting worse, into adult life.

Key characteristics

Children with juvenile arthritis may

- suffer from stiff and often painful joints, which inhibit their movements
- suffer from infections in their eyes
- have difficulties in concentrating and lack energy due to their medication, which has to be stronger during flares
- feel frustration, when in remission, at not being allowed to jump and climb when they want to in order to protect their vulnerable joints
- require daily physiotherapy, often more than once a day.

Support strategies

It will be important to follow medical advice and to work closely with the physiotherapist and the child's parents. Strategies at school may include

- exercises to flex and strengthen joints
- adapting PE sessions for the child so as to avoid movements which will aggravate the arthritis or put too much pressure on affected joints
- helping the child with any problematic activities, such as using scissors
- protecting the child at playtimes from others bumping into them or from falls
- ensuring that the child's parents are always notified if any classmates are suspected of having chickenpox or other illness that should be avoided.

Support agencies

- Arthritis Care
- Children's Chronic Arthritis Association (CCAA)
- Give Rheumatoid Arthritis Children Encouragement (GRACE)

Asperger syndrome

Children with Asperger syndrome display similar characteristics to those of autistic children. They have problems with communication, social relationships and making imaginative responses. However, they are often more articulate than autistic children and may be keen to speak at great length on their own personal topics of interest.

Children with Asperger syndrome may find any large group of people, including a room full of children, daunting and even threatening. They don't like to be the focus of others' attention and respond negatively, sometimes aggressively, to any situation they don't understand. When challenged they may seek to hide in a small, enclosed space such as a cupboard or a toilet cubicle.

Asperger syndrome requires a multi-professional diagnosis.

Key characteristics

Children with Asperger syndrome may

- have difficulty understanding jokes, idioms or figures of speech – everything is taken literally, making it difficult for them to make friends, understand some oral instructions and follow parts of the literacy hour

- respond aggressively

- find it hard to interpret body language and facial expressions

- tend to avoid eye contact

- seem to respond inappropriately to other people's feelings, due to a lack of awareness of others' emotions or reactions

- become obsessively interested in a hobby and/or be especially talented at something like music or art

- tend to talk obsessively about topics of their own interest in an expressionless tone of voice

- need to follow routines exactly, to the point where they become rituals, and be very upset at any changes in normal home or school routines

- follow any instruction or statement literally

- have difficulty thinking in abstract terms

- find it hard to make and keep friends because they have difficulty relating to the needs of others

- feel aggravated and confused by the brightness or buzzing sound of some types of lighting.

Support strategies

You may need to

- provide an area in the classroom where they can have their own personal space and avoid distractions, perhaps facing the wall and possibly screened off

- ensure that the classroom has an element of continuity – not too many changes at one time

- prepare them well in advance for any changes in school routine, if possible, as this can be very distressing for them

- use a daily visual timetable for younger children

- keep instructions clear and simple, checking that they understand by repeating the instructions to them individually as they do not understand that general instructions are for them unless their name is used

- use ICT to support their learning in a variety of ways

- use visual and concrete materials to support understanding of conceptual vocabulary

- explain jokes, idioms and figures of speech

- teach children how to interpret social signals eg. facial expression, gestures

- use games and activities to teach social conventions and interaction eg. turn-taking

- give them the opportunity to explain their anxieties

- give a logical explanation when asking them to do something new

- ensure that they understand that school and classroom rules apply to them

- speak to them in a calm and motionless manner.

Support agencies

- National Autistic Society

- Online Asperger Syndrome Information and Support (OASIS)

Asthma

Children with asthma have airways that narrow and can become clogged with mucus as a reaction to various triggers. When a child comes into contact with something which irritates their airways (a trigger), this sets off an attack and they find it difficult to breathe. Triggers vary between individuals, but common triggers include

- viral infections such as colds or flu
- allergies such as grass, pollen, animal fur and house dust mites
- irritants such as cold air or passive smoking.

It is important that children themselves, as well as school staff, know what their individual triggers may be.

Exercise, particularly in cold, dry weather and anxiety or stress can sometimes bring on attacks. Children with asthma are likely to have fewer attacks if they are fit, so they need to be encouraged to take part in regular exercise. However the type, duration and strenuousness of exercise may need to be adapted to suit their particular condition.

Most children with asthma will have fewer symptoms as they grow older through their teenage years, but it can continue or return in adulthood.

Neither the asthma itself nor the medication should have any direct effect on the child's learning and concentration. However, the anxiety caused by the asthma symptoms, the frequently interrupted sleep patterns and the severity of simple ailments when exacerbated by asthma can make the child very tired and may therefore affect their energy and concentration levels at school and when doing homework.

Key characteristics

Children with asthma may

- have difficulty in breathing, especially in breathing out
- wheeze on breathing out
- become breathless during or after exercise
- have a persistent cough, with coughing fits during attacks
- seem excessively tired or lethargic
- complain of a tight chest or a tummy ache
- turn blue around the lips in a severe attack

- appear tired and listless if short of sleep
- seem anxious prior to an attack
- seem to suffer from more or worse colds and minor illnesses than most children.

Support strategies

During an attack you need to

- encourage them to breathe deeply and slowly
- ensure that they are sitting rather than lying down
- remain calm and encourage them to calm down and relax as much as possible
- help them to relieve their symptoms with medication, using an inhaler, repeating after five minutes if it is not effective the first time
- help younger children to use a spacer device
- call an ambulance if the medication has no effect after five to ten minutes or if the child appears very distressed.

At all times you will need to

- ensure that all inhalers are marked with the child's name and take them outside during PE sessions or other outdoor activities
- give some leeway with homework deadlines if it has been a bad week
- allow the child to stay inside during breaktimes on very cold days
- help the child to avoid or minimise anxiety.

Support agencies

- National Asthma Campaign

Attention deficit/hyperactivity disorder (ADD/ADHD)

The terms ADD and ADHD are medical diagnoses and describe a syndrome of emotional or behavioural difficulties, which may include extreme impulsiveness, inattentiveness and continuous motor activity. There are two subgroups of childhood ADD.

- **ADHD** – the impulsive-hyperactive type.
- **ADD** – without hyperactivity – the inattentive-impulsive type.

This is a complex condition. Children with ADD or ADHD may sometimes be on medication which the school may be asked to administer during the day. More boys than girls seem to be affected.

Key characteristics

A child with ADD or ADHD may

- display impulsivity in all areas of school life
- murmur, talk or call out continuously because they are unable to internalise speech
- get up and wander around
- lash out physically or verbally with no thought for the consequences
- be easily distracted and therefore find it hard to focus on one activity
- avoid tasks that require sustained attention
- often move from one incomplete activity to another
- find it hard to make and keep friends
- find it hard to follow instructions
- often make mistakes because of an inability to attend to detail
- have poor organisational and self-help skills eg. getting dressed, finding tools for a task
- forget daily routines
- be unable to concentrate during tasks involving turn-taking
- be unaware of danger when running and climbing
- have constant fidgety movement of hands and feet
- have difficulty in waiting and allowing others to take turns in a game.

Support strategies

You may need to

- be consistent in using an organised set of rules and routines, but make sure that the child is notified of any changes in routine well in advance
- praise small achievements and set up an agreed reward system for good behaviour rather than using too many sanctions for inappropriate behaviour
- provide opportunities for children to move in the classroom eg. brain gym, practical activities and responsibilities
- explain to others that it is the behaviour that is a problem, not the child as a person
- use time out as a benefit rather than a sanction, as a time to calm down and be away from distractions
- try to use direct eye contact when talking to the child
- give short, simple instructions and encourage the child to talk through a task before attempting it
- let the child work in an individual or paired situation rather than expecting them to work in a group
- teach social skills – don't expect the child to pick up acceptable social behaviour
- focus on effort rather than achievement
- be realistic in your expectations – set short, clearly-defined targets.

Support agencies

- ADD/ADHD Family Support Group
- ADD Information Services (ADDISS)
- ADDNET UK

Autistic spectrum disorder (ASD)

This condition affects a child's ability to socialise and to develop speech and language. The main characteristics are now commonly described as a triad of impairments. These impairments affect

- communication – language impairment, which may include speech, intonation, gesture, body language or facial expression
- social interaction – difficulties such as lack of empathy and perception, inappropriate eye-contact, poor grasp of timing or rejection of physical contact
- imaginative thought – inflexible or over-literal thought-processes, which may include obsessional behaviours or repetitive movements and a resistance to change.

Children with autism will experience many of the same difficulties as children with Asperger syndrome. These difficulties may range from mild to severe. Like Asperger syndrome, this condition requires a multi-disciplinary diagnosis. Children with autistic spectrum disorder will have a different view of the world and of what is important.

Key characteristics

Children with autistic spectrum disorder may

- find it hard or even impossible to look others in the eye
- prefer to be solitary, have great difficulty dealing with other children invading their personal space
- flap arms or hands, particularly when frustrated or upset
- have delayed speech – up to 50 per cent of autistic children have difficulty with developing spoken language
- have difficulty understanding jokes, idioms or figures of speech – everything is taken literally, making it difficult for them to make friends, understand some oral instructions and follow parts of the literacy hour
- have difficulties with language, such as parroting what others say, repeating one phrase over and over or speaking in a monotone
- fly into a rage for no apparent reason although this usually turns out to be because someone has moved something or changed a routine
- display repetitive behaviour, such as turning lights on and off, opening and closing doors, or watching the same videos over and over again.

Support strategies

You may need to

- provide an area in the classroom where the child can have their own personal space, with the minimum of distractions
- ensure that the classroom has an element of continuity – not too many changes at one time
- prepare them well in advance for any changes in school routine, if possible, as this can be very distressing for them
- be consistent in the management of behaviour
- use a daily visual timetable for younger children
- use visual task lists for older children
- keep instructions clear and simple, checking that they understand by repeating the instructions to them individually as they will not understand that general instructions are for them unless their name is used
- use ICT to support their learning in a variety of ways
- explain jokes, idioms and figures of speech – what they are, what they mean and how they work
- teach the child how to interpret social signals
- use social stories to support a child in specific social situations
- teach self-help skills
- use visual and concrete materials to support understanding of conceptual vocabulary
- use games and activities to teach social conventions and interaction eg. turn-taking
- ensure that they understand that school and classroom rules apply to them.

Support agencies

- Autism Independent UK
- National Autistic Society

Brittle bones (osteogenesis imperfecta)

Brittle bones is a range of conditions which cause the bones to break very easily. Although children with brittle bones may not have learning difficulties, their medical condition will affect them at school and may make access to some areas of the National Curriculum more difficult. They may also have missed out on normal pre-school experiences, which may have delayed their learning in some ways.

It is important that children with brittle bones are helped to live as normal and independent a life as possible. There are different types of brittle bones and whilst some children may suffer relatively slightly, others will be severely affected, being of short stature and unable to walk. Some children may need to use walking-sticks, crutches or specialised wheelchairs in school. Physical alterations to the building may be needed.

In some children, fractures can be caused by everyday activities such as opening a door or picking something up. All staff need to be aware of procedures in case of a fracture.

Children with brittle bones often have joints in their hands that are affected by their condition and may need to change their writing hand or the way they hold a pencil. Whilst many forms of PE may be unsuitable for a child with brittle bones, swimming is a particularly good exercise and should be encouraged. Special toilet arrangements may be needed if the child uses a wheelchair or has shortened arms.

Key characteristics

A child with brittle bones may have

- frequent absences from school while fractures heal
- some learning delay as a result of physical problems eg. taking longer to learn to write
- difficulties with gross motor skills
- difficulties with fine motor skills
- some respiratory problems
- poor self-esteem and low self-confidence
- anxiety about their safety in the school environment.

Support strategies

You may need to

- liaise with hospital and home tuition services when necessary
- take advice from an occupational therapist to support the development of motor skills
- provide a writing slope if necessary
- provide a pencil-grip or experiment with different types of pen
- make special arrangements such as ICT for recording work if the writing arm or hand is fractured – a specially adapted computer keyboard or a voice-activated word-processor can be very useful in these situations
- make flexible arrangements for PE lessons and for playtimes if necessary
- use a buddy system for specific times of the day
- provide specialised training for a teaching assistant to help with lifting and to assist with using the toilet if necessary
- offer emotional support as the condition worsens – children may have to come to terms with using a wheelchair
- make use of circletime to talk about problems and/or provide an adult mentor
- organise physical access to different parts of the school if necessary
- ensure that appropriate adult support is provided at times of physical vulnerability
- encourage participation in all school activities as far as possible.

Support agencies

- Brittle Bone Society

Cerebral palsy

Cerebral palsy is the generic name for a group of disorders affecting muscles and movement. If, for any reason, the movement part of the brain is injured or fails to develop normally, the child may be born with or develop cerebral palsy. Approximately two people in every thousand have cerebral palsy. It neither worsens nor ameliorates, but stays at the same level throughout life. However, children can be taught strategies to deal with it and to develop as much independence as possible.

In a child with cerebral palsy, messages between the brain and the muscles are jumbled. There are three types of cerebral palsy, defined by which messages are affected. Many children with cerebral palsy have a combination of these three different types.

- **Spastic cerebral palsy** results in stiffening of the muscles and difficulty with joint movements. Even the simplest activities may be very difficult to do. If one side of the body is affected this is called hemiplegia. If the legs are the most affected it is called diplegia and if both arms and legs are affected it is called quadriplegia.

- **Athetoid cerebral palsy** results in involuntary movements as muscles tense and relax. Often these children have difficulty controlling their movements for breathing and speech. Hearing may also be affected.

- **Ataxic cerebral palsy** results in the whole body being affected. The child will probably be able to walk, but their balance and coordination will be affected. They will have jerky hand movements and speech.

An important fact to remember is that no two children with cerebral palsy are the same. Some are affected so mildly it's hardly noticeable at first, while in others the effects are immediately obvious.

Key characteristics

Some children with cerebral palsy may

- have very rigid limbs and limited or exaggerated movements
- have difficulty in walking and moving
- have either muscle weakness, stiffness, floppiness or spasms
- make involuntary movements as muscles tense and relax

- have difficulty talking or jerky speech
- have hearing difficulties
- have chewing and/or swallowing difficulties
- have epilepsy
- need help with self-care skills
- have difficulty distinguishing shapes (a problem with visual perception rather than eyesight) and may also have a squint
- have learning difficulties, sometimes related to a specific activity such as reading, drawing or maths
- have difficulties maintaining friendships if they cannot join in with other children's interests
- have poor self-esteem.

Support strategies

You may need to

- organise physical access to different parts of the school
- liaise on a regular basis with the relevant professionals
- ensure that appropriate adult support is provided
- make use of ICT as an aid to learning
- make use of audio-visual aids
- ensure that extra time is given for specific tasks
- adapt physical activities, especially PE
- use circletime to discuss inclusion issues for all the children in the class
- celebrate ability not disability – some children may be very able in a specific area.

Support agencies

- Capability Scotland
- Scope

Cleft lip or palate

Cleft is another word for split or separated. Parts of the face develop and join together during pregnancy and if this joining is incomplete the baby will have a cleft in their lip or palate.

A cleft lip is an opening between the nose and the mouth, which can be anything from a slight, almost imperceptible notch in the upper lip itself to a full separation running from the upper lip into the nose. A one-sided cleft is called a unilateral cleft. If the cleft is on both sides it is called a bilateral cleft.

A cleft palate affects the roof of the mouth and means that it is not fully joined together. This can range from a slight opening at the back of the soft palate, to a large separation the full length of the roof of the mouth.

A cleft lip will probably not cause any feeding problems in the baby, whereas a baby with a cleft palate will probably not be able to form a vacuum in its mouth and will therefore find it hard to suck or may have some other related problem. This may have knock-on effects in later childhood.

Specialists involved in supporting babies and children with cleft lips or palates may include a cleft nurse, an orthodontist, a surgeon, a paediatrician, a speech and language therapist and an educational psychologist.

While it is usually possible to repair a cleft lip during the first few months of a baby's life, treating a cleft palate is more complex. However, this can usually be done, at least partially, by the time the child is about a year old. In either case, if the repair has been successful, the child can usually develop reasonable speech, but may need help from the speech and language therapist to pronounce some sounds and to control nasal breathing.

Key characteristics

Children with cleft lip or palate may have

- external physical features which may affect the lip and the nose
- difficulty pronouncing some sounds
- a nasal tone when speaking
- difficulty in controlling the amount of air going into the nose
- hearing problems or glue ear
- regular absences for checks or treatment by the appropriate professionals

- a brace on the teeth, especially when the permanent teeth come through
- low self-esteem because the child looks different or speaks differently
- anxieties about being listened to and understood or about being teased or bullied
- difficulties in being understood by new people or in unfamiliar situations.

Support strategies

You may need to

- liaise regularly with all the relevant professionals
- listen carefully and attentively
- encourage the child to gain confidence talking and reading in a variety of situations
- encourage the child to speak more slowly if appropriate
- ensure that, if the child's hearing is weak, they sit near the teacher or speaker
- provide an adult mentor for them to talk through their anxieties and frustrations
- follow a programme of activities to strengthen and clarify different elements of speech.

Support agencies

- Cleft Lip and Palate Association (CLAPA)

Cystic fibrosis

Cystic fibrosis is a genetic disease that affects a number of organs in the body (especially the lungs and pancreas) by clogging them with thick, sticky mucus. This also affects the child's digestion. It is the UK's most common life-threatening childhood disease. Until the 1930s, babies born with cystic fibrosis rarely lived to be more than a few months old. Now, average life-expectancy is about 31 and rising. Most children with cystic fibrosis can expect to reach adulthood and enjoy active and fulfilling lives. Children with cystic fibrosis are academically as able as their peers, but hospitalisations and chest infections can result in frequent or prolonged absences from school.

Children with cystic fibrosis may be small and underweight for their age. A daily routine of physiotherapy and exercise is essential for every sufferer, to prevent irreparable lung damage. This can be very time-consuming and frustrating. Some children will also be embarrassed by having to have such arrangements made for them. Most children with cystic fibrosis will need to take medication (enzymes in the form of pills or powders) at mealtimes, too.

Some children with cystic fibrosis may develop diabetes, for which they might need to take insulin and moderate their diet. These children may also need to use the toilet more often.

Key characteristics

The most noticeable feature of cystic fibrosis is a persistent cough. Although not infectious, it may be embarrassing in front of other children, especially as a severe coughing attack occasionally leads to coughing up mucus or vomiting.

A child with cystic fibrosis may also suffer from

- repeated chest infections
- low resistance to all infections
- tendency to prolonged diarrhoea
- poor weight gain
- particularly salty sweat
- digestive problems
- lack or loss of energy
- frequent absences from school (sometimes prolonged).

Support strategies

You may need to

- make provision for daily physiotherapy in a quiet room with a dedicated teaching assistant who has been appropriately trained. Nebuliser treatment may also be necessary. The number of physiotherapy sessions that take place each day varies according to the child's current state of health. The length of each session will vary from 15 minutes to an hour
- ensure that special supplements are taken with all meals and snacks. These come in capsule form and need to be taken in large quantities
- provide work for the child to do at home or liaise with the hospital or home tuition service during prolonged absences
- encourage independence in taking responsibility for their own treatment (such as the taking of enzymes with food and pacing themselves during PE)
- encourage physical exercise, although the illness can result in energy loss and this must be taken into account during PE and other physical activities.

Support agencies

- Cystic Fibrosis Resource Centre
- Cystic Fibrosis Trust

Diabetes

This condition is a metabolic disorder in which a person's normal hormonal mechanisms do not control their blood sugar levels effectively. This causes the body to try to use fats as an alternative source of energy, with consequent effects. Diabetes can be caused by a number of factors, including stress.

When diabetes starts in childhood it is usually much more severe than when it begins in middle or old age. Most children with diabetes need two injections of insulin each day, which they usually administer themselves at home. Some will take medication instead and this may need to be taken at school. Treatment is based on a carefully controlled diet, with adequate amounts of carbohydrate, together with the drugs or insulin. Children with diabetes need to ensure that their blood glucose levels remain stable and may monitor their levels using a testing machine at regular intervals.

There are two main types of diabetes.

- **Diabetes insipidus** is a rare metabolic disorder which is due to a deficiency of the pituitary hormone which regulates the reabsorption of water in the kidneys.
- **Diabetes mellitus** is much more common, especially in children. It is a disorder of the carbohydrate metabolism in which sugars are not effectively converted to energy, causing raised sugar levels in the blood and urine.

If a child with diabetes misses a meal or a snack, takes the wrong amount of insulin or medication, or takes too much strenuous exercise, they may have a hypoglycaemic episode, or 'hypo'. Alternatively, a child may have an imbalance in the amount of insulin or medication they take due to an infection. This may lead to a diabetic coma. In both cases, it is essential to call the doctor immediately.

Key characteristics

A child with diabetes may

- lack energy
- lose weight
- suffer from dry skin and skin problems
- be excessively thirsty
- have a sore tongue
- have frequent pins and needles

- have blurred vision
- need to go to the toilet frequently to pass large quantities of dilute urine.

Indications of a hypo include

- excessive hunger
- sweating
- shaking or trembling
- irritability
- lack of concentration
- drowsiness
- pallor
- glazed eyes.

Indications of impending coma include

- loss of appetite
- nausea
- abdominal discomfort
- furred tongue
- drowsiness
- giddiness
- slow, deep breathing
- sweet-smelling breath
- flushed face.

Support strategies

You may need to

- allow the child to eat regularly during the day but particularly before exercise
- call the doctor or an ambulance immediately when the child is having a hypo or is in a coma
- give fast acting sugar (eg. glucose tablets, a sugary drink, a small chocolate bar) if they have a hypo
- give slower-acting starchy food (eg. sandwich, biscuits, milk) when they have recovered from a hypo (about 10–15 minutes later).

Support agencies

- Diabetes UK

Down syndrome

Down syndrome is a genetic condition whereby a child is born with an extra chromosome. The condition is usually detectable at birth. Children with Down syndrome have distinctive physical features. They often suffer from heart, breathing and eye problems and also have moderate to severe learning difficulties. This is a very wide spectrum. Some children will be able to have full access to and participation in the curriculum with appropriate levels of learning support. Others will have difficulties which prevent their prospering in a mainstream school for more than a year or two and will need close support in a special school or unit.

Children with Down syndrome are well known to be generally cheerful and loving. They can also be very active and lack any sense of danger or social propriety. A child with Down syndrome will normally need a dedicated teaching assistant to support their learning. However, they can also be helped to participate in group and class activities to great effect. They will need to be encouraged to develop independence gradually and not be over-supported in the primary years. Outreach can often be arranged with a nearby special school in order to support the mainstream school in giving the child with Down syndrome access to the curriculum.

Key characteristics

Children with Down syndrome may

- walk and talk much later than other children
- have some auditory and visual impairment
- develop more slowly physically and be relatively immature emotionally
- have delayed fine and gross motor skills
- be strong visual learners but poor auditory learners
- have significant speech and language delay, relative to their cognitive abilities
- have difficulties with short-term auditory memory and auditory processing
- have a short concentration span
- have difficulties with consolidation, retention, generalisation and transfer of skills
- have a tendency to avoidance strategies.

Support strategies

You may need to

- ensure that learning activities are broken down into small steps and are clearly focused
- provide a multisensory approach to learning
- provide activities to develop motor skills
- use visual and concrete materials to aid understanding
- keep language simple and familiar
- make use of songs, rhymes and rhythm to aid learning sequences eg. alphabet, days of the week
- keep instructions short and concise
- ask children to repeat instructions in order to clarify understanding
- vary the level of demand and type of support within a lesson
- allow time for children to process and respond to verbal input
- provide alternative methods of recording
- ensure repetition and reinforcement within a variety of contexts
- encourage participation in all school activities if possible
- encourage independence and self-help
- develop outreach liaison with a nearby special school
- monitor and record progress so that each small achievement is recognised.

Support agencies

- Down's Syndrome Association
- Down Syndrome Education Trust

Dyscalculia

Dyscalculia is a specific learning disability involving maths skills. It may be a difficulty with counting and calculating, understanding abstract maths concepts or working with numbers and symbols.

Key characteristics

Children with dyscalculia may have

- normal or above average verbal skills and a good visual memory for the printed word
- difficulty understanding maths concepts, rules and sequences, especially time and money
- a tendency to make substitutions, transpositions, omissions and reversals when reading and writing numbers
- a poor sense of direction (eg. confusing left and right, getting easily lost, losing things) and time (eg. often arriving late)
- difficulty recalling names and faces
- poor mental maths skills
- poor coordination when involved in activities requiring change of direction such as aerobics, exercise and dance sessions
- difficulty with keeping score in games or working out strategies in chess.

Support strategies

You may need to

- allow extra time to complete a task
- encourage children to make use of calculators when necessary
- use visual and concrete materials to develop an understanding of maths concepts
- make use of ICT as an aid to learning
- use multisensory teaching strategies to support the learning of new concepts
- encourage working with a partner to explain methods of working to each other
- incorporate practical activities into most lessons
- allow for the need to overlearn maths concepts and rules.

Support agencies

- Dyslexia Institute

Dysgraphia

Dysgraphia is a processing problem causing difficulty in remembering and using the correct sequence of muscle movements in order to write. It is a neurologically based difficulty and is often related to other specific learning difficulties. Dysgraphia is frustrating for children who have good oral language skills but are unable to transfer their ideas easily into written form.

Key characteristics

Children with dysgraphia may

- write slowly and laboriously, and have poor presentation
- have inconsistent letter formation and use a mixture of upper and lower case letters
- have difficulty with their pencil grip
- have difficulty with copying and taking notes
- use a rubber excessively
- have difficulty with directions eg. in map work, plans, diagrams.

Support strategies

You may need to

- teach the child keyboard skills as soon as possible and use a word-processor
- allow them to write seated in the position that suits them best
- allow them to write in the style and form that suits them best
- allow extra time for writing activities
- use planning and writing frames
- encourage the use of visual organisation strategies, such as mind-mapping
- develop alternative methods of recording eg. diagrams, posters, charts, comic strips
- allow the use of a scribe where appropriate
- give the child more opportunities to talk about their ideas rather than writing them.

Support agencies

- Dyslexia Institute

Dyslexia

Dyslexia is a specific learning difficulty that affects the ability to read and spell. About 60 per cent of children with dyslexia also have trouble with the sounds that make up words.

Dyslexia can also cause difficulties with basic maths (especially the order of numbers and multiplication tables), general literacy skills, word interpretation and perception, organisational skills, short-term memory, sequencing and processing information. Children with dyslexia, however, are often very creative and able in certain areas of the curriculum, such as art, design, technology, computing, drama and lateral thinking.

Dyslexia is a complex neurological disorder and affects about ten per cent of the population, across all levels of intellectual ability. It tends to affect boys more than girls and often runs in families. It is believed to have a genetic cause.

Key characteristics

A dyslexic child may

- use bizarre spellings and have poor phonological awareness
- frequently lose their place when reading and see blurred or distorted word-shapes
- confuse some high frequency words eg. was/saw
- reverse letters and number digits beyond the age where this is normal
- write words with the correct letters in the wrong order
- write sequences of letters and numbers in reverse
- have difficulty remembering a word and substitute other words instead
- have great difficulty organising themselves and their belongings
- be unable to remember simple sequences such as days of the week
- experience problems following oral instructions
- have poor senses of time and direction
- make frequent errors when copying, especially from the board
- have some coordination difficulties
- have low levels of motivation and self-esteem.

Support strategies

You may need to

- teach syllable count to help the child hear how many syllables are in a word
- teach how to blend syllables
- teach onset and rime to help the child to discriminate between words aurally
- teach phoneme discrimination to help the child identify phonemes in words
- teach phoneme-blending to help the child with reading and spelling
- use multisensory methods to support the child's learning
- ensure repetition of learning, using word and language games for enjoyment
- make use of coloured overlays and line trackers where necessary
- create a positive reading environment with opportunities to listen to stories
- teach keyboard skills and encourage use of spell-checkers
- encourage alternative methods of recording eg. writing-frames, diagrams, labelled drawings, flow charts, comic strip stories
- allow the use of a scribe where appropriate, especially for copying anything important such as homework instructions
- make use of audio-visual aids
- keep oral instructions brief and clear
- revise and review previously taught skills at frequent intervals
- raise self-esteem and confidence with lots of praise and encouragement.

Support agencies

- British Dyslexia Association
- British Dyslexics
- Dyslexia Institute

Dyspraxia (developmental coordination disorder)

Dyspraxia is a specific learning difficulty. Children with dyspraxia have problems with motor coordination and often appear clumsy when moving around the classroom. They have perceptual-motor problems and find writing difficult. They may also have pronunciation difficulties, caused by problems in controlling the movements of the mouth and the tongue. Developmental dyspraxia is suspected when it is obvious that the difficulties are not due to a medical condition.

Approximately one child in 20 suffers from this condition, which affects four times as many boys as girls.

Key characteristics

Children with dyspraxia may

- appear to be clumsy, bumping into people and objects
- have difficulty in judging distances and the position of objects in space, so find ball games particularly hard
- be unable to change speed and direction without overbalancing
- need to be watched carefully when climbing on playground equipment because they have no sense of danger
- appear to be uncoordinated, particularly when running, jumping, hopping or riding a bike
- be unsure of which hand to use and may change hands in the middle of an activity
- have immature use of pencils, crayons, scissors, puzzles and simple construction toys
- have difficulty in copying shapes and pictures
- have difficulty producing some speech sounds and be unable to communicate their ideas easily
- find it confusing if they are given too much verbal information at a time because they take longer to process it and are rarely able to make immediate responses
- find it hard to sequence information and reproduce it verbally, which affects their ability to answer questions in the classroom
- find it difficult to adapt to a structured school routine
- have limited concentration and poor listening skills

- be easily upset and have temper tantrums – which annoys other children
- have poor social interactions and difficulty making friends
- be rough and aggressive because they have difficulty controlling their movements.

Support strategies

You may need to

- give clear, simple instructions and constant reminders, both oral and written
- provide a reasonably quiet working environment
- organise activities to develop listening and attention skills such as sound tapes
- encourage children to present ideas using ICT
- incorporate suggested motor coordination exercises into a PE programme
- organise games and activities requiring cooperation and turn-taking
- practise a range of sequencing activities eg. pictorial activity and story sequences, word and sentence sequences, days, months and number sequences
- develop role-play and drama activities, including puppets
- help children organise their written work by using writing frames
- give clear, simple instructions with frequent reminders but avoid nagging
- praise every effort and successful achievement of new skills
- practise tracking activities eg. mazes, dot-to-dot, tracing, letter shapes.

Support agencies

- Dyscovery Centre
- Dyspraxia Foundation

Emotional and behavioural difficulties (EBD)

This term is used when a child's ongoing behavioural difficulties appear to have their root cause in emotional or possibly social problems. It is important to remember that some children have such deep-rooted emotional difficulties that these may manifest themselves in unusual quietness, rather than disruptive behaviour.

Some emotional and behavioural problems may be temporary and can be dealt with using standard pastoral strategies. But others are so complex that outside professionals need to be involved to help the child cope with daily living and learning.

A variety of praise and reward strategies are often useful and it is important to raise self-esteem at every opportunity. It may also be helpful to consider making a home visit or to arrange to see the parents in school and involve them in agreeing a home-school programme of action.

It is advisable to consider the wellbeing of all the other children in the class, as well as any adults who work with a child with emotional and behavioural difficulties.

Key characteristics

Children with emotional and behavioural difficulties may

- find it difficult to form friendships
- often appear preoccupied and therefore find it difficult to get involved in activities
- have difficulty keeping on task
- have difficulty taking part in group activities and discussion
- often become tearful or throw tantrums for no apparent reason
- have psychosomatic illnesses
- have low self-esteem and often become victims of bullies
- become bullies themselves
- be aggressive and disruptive
- find it difficult to conform to classroom rules and routines
- be excessively attention-seeking through either negative behaviour or clinginess
- sometimes have school phobia
- underachieve in many areas of the school curriculum.

Support strategies

You may need to

- ensure a consistent approach to the child's behavioural difficulties by all members of staff by developing positive behaviour-management strategies
- encourage the provision of a positive classroom environment
- have group and class discussions (circletime) to focus on problems and give all childen opportunities to air their views in a controlled environment
- set up small social skills groups for children who have difficulties in particular areas such as relating to other children or anger management
- develop social interaction through games and paired problem-solving activities
- give short, clearly-defined tasks
- encourage the development of ICT skills to increase motivation
- provide activities that encourage the building of self-esteem
- give the child opportunities to express their feelings through the use of puppets or role-play in pairs or small groups
- develop positive links between older and younger children
- arrange for educational psychologist or behavioural support input such as circle of friends, if appropriate
- arrange for counselling or family support provision usually through either the Educational Welfare Service, the Family Centre or the Child and Adult Mental Health service.

Support agencies

- Association of Workers for Children with Emotional and Behavioural Difficulties (AWCEBD)
- Contact-a-Family
- WATCh (What About The Children?)
- Young Minds

Epilepsy

Epilepsy is neither an illness or a disease, but rather a tendency of the brain to be triggered to cause a spasm, a seizure or a fit, when neurones malfunction temporarily. Children with epilepsy have recurrent seizures or fits, the great majority of which can be controlled by medication. Seizures may be partial (where the child doesn't lose consciousness) or generalised (where the child does lose consciousness). The seizures can vary from major attacks which involve the whole brain to very minor, momentary 'absences'.

- **Generalised seizures** may take the form of major convulsions, with jerking of the limbs, either stiffness or floppiness and unconsciousness. Breathing will probably be noisy and irregular and there may be involuntary incontinence.

- **Partial seizures** are caused by a local disturbance in the brain. The type of seizure experienced will depend on which area of the brain is involved. The seizures can vary from very mild and momentary absences which give the impression of daydreaming, with perhaps a slight twitching of an arm or leg and odd sensations or tastes, to general confusion in which the child appears dazed and detached from their surroundings. Children suffering partial epileptic seizures rarely lose consciousness, but will probably not be aware of the moments when the seizure was happening.

- **Photosensitive epilepsy** is quite rare and usually occurs as a result of being in a room where there is strobe lighting, which can trigger a seizure in this type of epilepsy.

Epilepsy usually starts either in infancy or in adolescence. If it starts at another time, it may be as a result of a head injury, infection, stroke or tumour. It can be life-long or experienced over a relatively short period of time (anything from two or three years upwards).

Key characteristics

Children with epilepsy may

- be more inclined to have a seizure through illness, lack of sleep, flickering lights, stress, certain food allergies

- suffer from lapsed concentration and attention

- have problems if the frequency of fits and recovery time causes breaks from learning

- demonstrate anxiety if an attack feels imminent

- feel embarrassed and self-conscious

- need emotional support to deal with the condition and any teasing

- be nervous about swimming lessons

- be lethargic or aggressive or suffer mood changes, any of which may be a clue that medication needs adjusting.

Support strategies

You may need to

- ensure close supervision when children are climbing, swimming or undertaking any other potentially hazardous activity

- check with parents about factors that are known to trigger seizures

- alert staff to any child who may have absences

- ensure that all staff know what to do if a seizure takes place.

During a seizure, you should not

- move a child, unless they are in a dangerous place

- restrain them or put anything in their mouth

- give them anything to drink.

During a seizure, you should

- respond calmly and calm down other children and adults

- ensure other children don't crowd around

- put something soft under the child's head and maintain their airway

- call an ambulance if the seizure lasts longer than usual, or if you are in any doubt

- when the convulsion has stopped, put the child on one side in the recovery position.

Support agencies

- British Epilepsy Association

- Epilepsy Action

Fragile X syndrome

Fragile X is thought to be the most common inherited form of learning disability. It is usually caused by an X chromosome that carries a mutation of a particular gene. It is a genetic defect and may be inherited. Fragile X is twice as common in boys as in girls and its effects are milder in girls. It is thought that this is because girls have two X chromosomes and that one can perhaps compensate for the other.

Fragile X affects behaviour, emotions, learning, speech and language. The range of effects is great and it is not possible to predict which of the many potential difficulties a child with fragile X will have. Indeed, it is possible for a child to have the damaged gene and yet not be affected by it at all. Children with fragile X often have high verbal abilities and have a good sense of humour. It is important however to ensure that the child with fragile X is not subjected to too many environmental stimuli (eg. sounds, movements, smells) at once. Children with fragile X are sometimes given medication to improve their concentration.

Key characteristics

A child with fragile X syndrome may

- repeat words and phrases, or the last words in a sentence, over and over
- fail to respond to direct questions
- give answers not obviously related to the question
- speak in rapid bursts
- have poor fine and gross motor coordination
- dislike work based on writing
- find large, noisy, unstructured group times distressing
- find it easier to learn in the morning, after a settling-in period
- become distressed by eye contact, touch, questioning in front of others
- react badly to pressures of time
- be oversensitive to relatively minor upsets and/or have disruptive outbursts
- prefer practical, physical activities
- have slight motor coordination problems
- enjoy repetitive tasks, which may have a calming effect
- have subtle physical characteristics, such as a large head, long face, large jaw, protruding ears, high palate or dental overcrowding.

Support strategies

You may need to

- provide as much positive attention as possible
- have an organised set of routines and make sure that the child is notified of any changes in these routines well in advance
- set up an agreed reward system for good behaviour, rather than using too many sanctions for inappropriate behaviour
- reward specific behaviours and explain this clearly
- praise every small achievement
- make use of visual clues
- give short, simple instructions – for complex tasks, give only one or two instructions at a time
- be consistent in the use of rules and routines
- let children work in an individual or paired situation, rather than expecting them to work in groups
- be realistic in your expectations, setting short, clearly defined targets.

Support agencies

- Fragile X Society (UK)
- National Fragile X Foundation (US)

Glue ear (otitis media)

Glue ear involves inflammation, either chronic or acute, and an accumulation of fluid in the middle ear. It can cause pain and hearing impairment. If it persists, an ear, nose and throat specialist will advise a simple operation to put in grommets to allow fluid to drain from the middle ear.

A large number of primary school children suffer from glue ear, especially when colds, flu and other minor infections and childhood diseases are present. The symptoms usually recur on a regular basis, particularly when the child has had a cold or throat infection which has infected the ear. If the problem is considered to be severe then antibiotics will be prescribed, and possibly decongestant nasal drops.

Otitis media is closely related to otitis externa, which is also known as swimmer's ear. This is an inflammation of the canal joining the ear-drum to the external ear, with similar effects.

If a child exhibits severe pain and distress at school and you suspect that it may be due to an ear infection, it is essential to speak to their parents and advise a visit to the doctor straight away. If left untreated or not treated early enough, ear infections associated with glue ear can cause permanent deafness or mastoiditis, which can lead to a brain abscess.

Key characteristics

A child who suffers with glue ear may

- talk loudly and be unaware of the level of their voice
- have poor listening and attention skills
- experience difficulties with developing phonological skills
- often appear to be withdrawn or in a world of their own
- have difficulties interacting with more than one or two people at a time
- be unable to participate fully in group activities
- need to have the sound on the television or radio at a higher level
- need to have instructions repeated clearly and slowly
- find it difficult to participate in music or singing lessons

- put their hands to their ears or head quite frequently (very young children may cry out with the pain)
- have frequent ear, nose and throat infections.

Support strategies

Always alert the parents if you are concerned about a child's hearing as this is a medical condition and needs parental action. Within school it is important to support children with glue ear by

- speaking slowly and clearly, but not necessarily more loudly
- allowing the child to sit where they can see your face
- making sure that you use the child's name to attract their attention
- having a low level of background noise in the classroom when you are giving direct teaching to the child's group
- providing opportunities for the child to work with a partner rather than in a group
- giving short, clear instructions.

Support agencies

- Hearing Research Trust

Hearing impairment

There are two types of hearing impairment or loss – conductive and sensori-neural. Some children can suffer from both conditions at the same time.

- **Conductive hearing loss** is commonly known as glue ear and is very common in young children after colds and/or earache. Most children outgrow this problem by the time they are seven years old.

- **Sensori-neural hearing loss** is much less common than the conductive type. It's caused by damage to the hearing mechanism itself – usually in the cochlea or along the nerve to the brain. Sensori-neural losses are found in four or five children per thousand with one or two of these cases being described as profound. This type of loss is permanent. It can range from mild to profound in degree and is unlikely to be corrected surgically. Early diagnosis of this type of loss is crucial in order to cut down the long-term effects on the child's language and speech development.

Most children with hearing impairment in mainstream education have a moderate to severe hearing loss. Some children will have been equipped with a hearing aid and possibly with a box for the teacher to wear to conduct the sound more clearly. Some mainstream schools have a hearing impaired unit.

Key characteristics

Children with a hearing impairment may

- rely on visual cues and lip-reading
- have some speech and language difficulties
- need ongoing support from a speech and language therapist
- need ongoing support from the local hearing impaired service
- need to wear a hearing aid
- have difficulties with hearing when there is background noise in the classroom
- misunderstand instructions and appear to copy others
- need to use some sign language
- have difficulty following radio and television programmes.

Support strategies

In a mainstream school you may need to

- seek the guidance and support of the hearing impaired service
- seek the guidance and support of the speech and language therapist
- be aware that the child will need to be seated where they can see the teacher clearly
- keep background noise to a minimum
- be familiar with the type of hearing aid the child is wearing
- speak clearly, but with no exaggeration of lip patterns
- simplify your statements and, if necessary, rephrase a sentence if it is obvious that the child has not understood
- use facial expressions to convey clues to what you are saying
- learn some basic sign language
- use Teletext subtitles when watching television programmes
- modify tasks to suit the language level of the child
- teach other children ways to communicate with the hearing-impaired child.

Support agencies

- British Association of Teachers of the Deaf (BATOD)
- British Deaf Association (BDA)
- Deaf Education through Listening and Talking (DELTA)
- Friends for the Young Deaf (FYD)
- RNID

Heart disorders

Most children with heart disorders have a congenital condition which means that the disorder has been present since birth. Although about half of these children will need an operation to improve their condition, some defects will correct themselves, whilst others are relatively minor and do not cause any great problems. Heart disease may be acquired as a result of rheumatic fever, but this is rare.

Because there is a huge range of degree and complexity in congenital heart conditions, each child is different in how he or she is affected and what they can or cannot do. Most children can lead ordinary lives, and can be allowed to limit their own activities without restraint from an adult. They need to learn to become independent and to understand and deal with their own condition.

Some children will be taking medicine. Most medicines have no obvious effects at school. However, if a child is taking medicine to help their body get rid of excess fluid, they will probably need more frequent and possibly more urgent trips to the toilet. Children who are in danger from blood clots take blood-thinning medicines, which prevent them from taking part in contact sports.

Key characteristics

Children with heart disorders may

- have poor physical development
- tire more quickly than other children
- need to limit the extent of their physical activity
- exhibit rapid breathing
- become breathless and, in some cases, their lips and skin may become blue
- have a lower tolerance to cold weather than other children (mainly because they cannot run around frequently to keep warm)
- have more severe reactions than other children to common infections like colds
- have more frequent absences than other children because of illness
- have some attention and concentration problems
- have difficulties with appetite and eating
- need support with self-help skills, and encouragement to become as independent as possible.

Support strategies

You may need to

- have regular liaison with parents to ensure that all medical needs are being met at school
- liaise with hospital and home tuition services when necessary
- encourage classmates to keep in touch when children are in hospital through cards, letters, jokes, photographs, etc.
- make flexible arrangements for PE lessons and for playtimes if necessary
- use a buddy system for rest times
- make use of circletime to talk about problems or, if preferred, offer the support of an adult mentor
- ensure that appropriate adult support is provided when necessary
- provide an adult mentor with whom the child may discuss anxieties and frustrations
- encourage participation in all school activities where possible
- ensure that extra time is given for specific tasks
- inform all staff about the child's conditions and alert them to symptoms which would indicate a potentially serious situation
- contact parents and call an ambulance if the child's condition suddenly deteriorates.

Support agencies

- Association for Children with Heart Disorders
- Children's Heart Federation

HIV (human immunodeficiency virus) and AIDS (acquired immune deficiency syndrome)

HIV is a virus that prevents the immune system from working properly, making it less effective at fighting infections. AIDS is the term used when loss of or damage to immune function caused by HIV has been diagnosed.

HIV and AIDS are not in themselves illnesses with their own set of symptoms, but rather they facilitate the development of infections and tumours because of the lack of immunity. The rate at which HIV or AIDS develops and the ways in which it affects the child will differ from case to case. It is therefore not possible to predict how either condition will develop for any particular child.

Although it is likely that a child with HIV will eventually develop AIDS, it is becoming increasingly likely that a child born HIV positive or who becomes HIV positive in infancy may live well into at least the teenage years.

It is important to understand that HIV cannot be transmitted by coughing, sneezing, touching or hugging. Children are far more at risk from catching a range of infectious diseases from each other than of developing HIV from having casual contact with a child who has been diagnosed as being HIV positive. Most schools try to minimise the risk of spreading infectious diseases by using agreed precautions and attending to proper hygiene for all children.

Children who have been born with HIV/AIDS should be able to attend mainstream school without fear of discrimination. However, many children may have already lost one or both of their parents to the virus and their relatives or carers may prefer to keep the diagnosis to themselves, so schools are often not informed of the situation.

Key characteristics

Children who are born with HIV/AIDS may have no symptoms at first. These usually appear within two to three years. They will have enlarged lymph nodes (glands of the immune system). They may also

- have frequent and severe bacterial infections
- be particularly susceptible to all childhood illnesses and infections
- experience loss of weight

- have a slow rate of growth
- develop rashes and other skin conditions
- lack energy and appear pale and lethargic.

Support strategies

If you know that a child has HIV/AIDS you may need to

- ensure that the child lives as normal a school life as possible
- liaise closely with the parents or carers about the child's knowledge and understanding of the disease and the possible outcomes
- provide training in appropriate procedures and related advice for all staff
- inform parents or carers immediately when there is an infectious disease in the school
- suggest activities the parents may do with the child when they are unable to attend school
- provide an adult mentor if the parents or carers feel that their child needs someone to talk to about their situation and the difficulties it can cause for them
- agree a plan with the headteacher and the class teacher as to how the school would deal with a case of unfavourable publicity and/or other parents' concerns.

Support agencies

- National AIDS Trust

Hydrocephalus

Hydrocephalus is a condition in which a watery fluid is produced continuously throughout the brain. This fluid is known as cerebro-spinal fluid and it normally flows from the brain, down the spinal cord and into the bloodstream. If any of the pathways are blocked, the fluid accumulates in the brain, causing it to swell. In babies and infants this causes the head to enlarge, but in older children the bones of the skull are fused and the head size cannot increase, which creates increasing pressure. Usually, a child with hydrocephalus has a shunt surgically inserted and this will drain the fluid and reduce the pressure from day to day.

Hydrocephalus can be present at birth or it can develop following a premature birth. Most children with spina bifida suffer from hydrocephalus. Hydrocephalus can also develop following meningitis, a stroke, a brain haemorrhage or a brain tumour.

Children with hydrocephalus can have fits, but these are not usually directly a result of the hydrocephalus, but rather of the condition which caused the pathways to become blocked. A child with hydrocephalus is likely to have learning difficulties or physical effects. This will vary from child to child and may be very slight.

Key characteristics

A child with hydrocephalus may

- have learning difficulties of various kinds
- have poor concentration, reasoning and short-term memory
- have co-ordination problems, especially eye-hand coordination and a degree of clumsiness
- have problems with motivation and organisational skills
- demonstrate sequencing difficulties
- have visual problems
- become seriously distressed by everyday noises
- suffer impaired vision (and possibly have their eyes fixed in a downward position, as a result of the cerebro-spinal fluid causing pressure on the nerves which control eye movement)
- develop breathing, speaking or swallowing difficulties
- have an early puberty.

Although a shunt usually works without any problems and is intended to last for a lifetime, it may possibly develop a blockage or an infection, or the tube may require surgically lengthening as the child grows. It is important to notice any sudden changes and to notify the parents straight away, or call the doctor or an ambulance if you feel particularly concerned. Signs of a blocked or infected shunt are

- general fatigue
- visual problems
- behavioural changes
- sudden or gradual decline in attainment levels
- vomiting
- headaches
- dizziness
- sensitivity to light
- drowsiness
- fits.

Support strategies

You may need to

- develop the child's concentration skills
- break instructions down into short sentences for everyday tasks
- teach simple sequencing activities
- develop strategies for improving short-term memory
- support the child in working on their coordination skills (especially eye to hand)
- develop strategies to help the child improve organisational skills
- adapt materials for a child who may have visual problems
- build confidence and self-esteem through encouragement and praise
- seek specialist advice for anything which causes concern.

Support agencies

- The Association for Spina Bifida and Hydrocephalus (ASBAH)

Leukaemia and cancer

One third of all cases of childhood cancer are leukaemia, which is a disease of the white blood cells. Leukaemia cells multiply in the bone marrow and normal cell production slows down. Childhood cancer affects about 1 in 650 children and around 60 per cent of these children can be cured and live normal lives.

Key characteristics

Children with cancer may

- have repeated infections
- lack appetite and suffer from weight-loss
- tire easily and need frequent rest
- have swollen glands
- need regular treatment which may cause side effects.

Support strategies

You may need to

- ensure that the child lives as normal a school life as possible
- liaise closely with the parents about their child's understanding of the disease and its progress
- inform parents immediately when there is an infectious disease in the school, as some cancer treatments can reduce the child's resistance to infection
- provide an adult mentor if the parents feel that their child needs someone to talk to about their situation.

Support agencies

- Cancer and Leukaemia in Childhood Trust (CLIC)
- Leukaemia Care Society
- Sargent Cancer Care for Children

ME (Myalgic encephalomyelitis or encephalopathy)

ME is a chronic disabling illness of the immune and central nervous system that affects children as well as adults. It is also known as chronic fatigue syndrome or post-viral fatigue syndrome. The cause is unclear but in many cases ME starts after a viral illness or after severe stress. The main symptom is fatigue following minimal physical or mental exertion. ME can last for up to three years.

Key characteristics

A child with ME may

- have severe muscle or joint pain and headaches that don't respond to painkillers
- have erratic sleep patterns (sometimes sleeping all the time or hardly at all)
- have a sore throat and/or enlarged lymph glands
- suffer with skin rashes or numbness
- feel sensitivity to noise, bright light and hot or cold temperatures
- lose their appetite and have some bowel problems
- suffer loss of concentration and have short-term memory and word-finding difficulties
- become irritable and frustrated
- have problems coping with any physical activity eg. walking, writing, speaking, singing.

Support strategies

Children who are severely affected will often need home tuition until they improve sufficiently to make a phased return to school.

You may need to

- offer part-time attendance at school
- facilitate regular rest periods in a quiet place
- provide an adult mentor to listen to the child's anxieties
- use circletime to talk about issues surrounding ME
- ensure that classroom tasks are short and clearly defined
- make flexible arrangements for PE lessons and for playtimes if necessary.

Support agencies

- Action for ME (AfME)
- Association of Young People with ME (AYME)
- ME Association

Moderate learning difficulties (MLD)

Children with moderate learning difficulties (also known as global learning difficulties) have a general developmental delay. They have difficulties with learning across all areas of the school curriculum. Children with MLD comprise the largest group of children with special educational needs in mainstream schools. Many of these children have a delay of about three years and consequently need a high level of support within the mainstream classroom.

Many children with moderate learning difficulties will also be suffering from low levels of self-esteem and motivation. They may become resentful and refuse to attempt new work as they perceive themselves to be likely to fail before they start. It is likely that they will become over-reliant on teaching assistants to help them with tasks and they will need much encouragement and praise to persuade them to attempt new challenges which are within their capability and develop greater independence.

Key characteristics

Children with MLD may

- have immature listening/attention skills
- have immature social skills
- rely on a teaching assistant to direct them within the class situation
- have a poor auditory memory
- have a poor visual memory
- have difficulty acquiring basic literacy and numeracy skills
- have difficulties with comprehension skills
- need a high level of support with investigation and problem-solving activities
- have poor verbal and non-verbal reasoning skills
- have difficulties with applying what they know to other situations
- have some motor coordination difficulties.

Support strategies

You may need to

- provide teaching assistant support at the beginning and end of a lesson, but encourage children to work independently whenever possible
- ensure that learning activities are broken down into small steps and are clearly focused
- simplify, differentiate or abbreviate class tasks

- provide a multisensory approach to learning
- provide activities to develop motor skills
- use visual and concrete materials to aid understanding
- keep language simple and familiar in guided group work
- make use of songs, rhymes and rhythm to aid learning sequences (eg. alphabet, days of the week)
- keep instructions short and concise
- ask children to repeat instructions in order to clarify understanding
- provide alternative methods of recording eg. labelled pictures, diagrams, flow charts
- ensure repetition and reinforcement within a variety of contexts
- allow extra time to complete a task
- monitor and record progress so that each small achievement is recognised
- organise activities to develop listening and attention skills eg. sound tapes
- practise a range of sequencing activities eg. pictorial activity or story sequences, word and sentence sequences, days, months and number sequences
- develop role play and drama activities including the use of finger and hand puppets to aid the understanding of new concepts
- help children organise their written work by using writing frames
- praise every effort and successful achievement of new skills.

Support agencies

- National Pyramid Trust

School phobia

Most children have days when they do not want to go to school, but school phobia is more serious than this. It can be identified as a persistent and frequent fear of attending school. It is often emotional in origin and is usually a social anxiety. Children with school phobia are just as likely to come from normal, happy families as any other children, and have the full range of abilities. Those children who seem to be most at risk are children who either have had a chronic illness, are the youngest child in the family or are only children.

When school phobia is suspected, an educational psychologist should be asked to make the diagnosis and will then help the child, parents and teachers to draw up a programme to reintegrate the child with school life. The local educational welfare officer is also likely to be closely involved. This is a difficult condition, but it is imperative to set up a programme of action at the earliest possible stage to ensure that the child doesn't develop too rigid an attitude. It is also essential that the school be as sympathetic to the problem as possible. The child is rarely being deliberately negative – they probably want to conform with their peers and settle back into school too, but anxiety repeatedly gets the better of them.

Key characteristics

A child with school phobia may

- have a fear of being away from home
- feel unhappy in social groups of more than five or six people
- fear what other children's reactions and questions will be if they do return to school and how they will answer them
- have low confidence and self-esteem and hate being the centre of attention
- complain of a range of illnesses eg. headache, fatigue, sickness, diarrhoea, dizziness
- have a fear of something tragic happening to a family member while they are at school
- be shy and emotionally immature.

Support strategies

You may need to

- work closely with the education welfare officer and the educational psychologist
- discuss the possible reasons for the child's anxiety with the parents
- liaise with the outside agencies who may be counselling both the child and their family
- provide reassurance and encouragement when the child is brought to school
- go into the classroom with the child to support them and to divert attention from them if they return to school during a lesson time
- avoid the settings and situations that cause anxiety eg. pre-empt or deflect the other children's questions or help the child know how to answer them without prompting too many more
- encourage the child to deal with their anxieties when they feel ready to do so
- provide a quiet, familiar place where the child can go when they feel anxious
- create familiar routines and encourage the child to take part in some of them
- provide an adult mentor to listen to the child and encourage them to talk about their anxieties
- provide activities for the child to do at home when necessary, but ask the parents to encourage the child to bring the completed activities into school
- give lots of praise and warm encouragement at every opportunity.

Support agencies

- National Phobics Society

Selective mutism

Children with selective mutism are physically capable of normal speech and comprehension but choose not to speak in certain situations. They may speak, but only in a whisper. Other children will often volunteer to speak for them. Selective mutism is not the same as mutism. Children diagnosed with mutism speak to no one.

There are several reasons why children may not speak and it is important that a speech and language therapist should investigate a variety of factors, before deciding on the approaches that would best support the child. Factors that cause selective mutism are often anxiety-related. Sometimes it will be a reaction to trauma of some kind. Occasionally it will be because the child suffers from a hearing impairment and therefore lacks the confidence to speak, except to a few familiar people. Children with selective mutism will sometimes speak to friends or siblings but not to adults. Most children with the condition make school their silent place.

When a child has chosen to be silent with adults in school, it is difficult to assess their attainment and progress, especially with reading. Situations may also arise when the child's selective mutism can make it more difficult or even dangerous for them, such as in the case of illness or injury. It will help if there is one adult, or perhaps a classmate, to whom the child is willing to speak in such circumstances.

Key characteristics

Children with selective mutism may

- have a fear of people, especially unknown adults
- speak at home with family and close relatives
- be overwhelmingly shy
- find eye-contact uncomfortable
- be expressionless and even rigid most of the time
- remain detached and on the edge of things
- have undiagnosed, intermittent or ongoing hearing problems
- feel unable to speak in social situations outside the home.

Support strategies

You may need to

- provide continuous reassurance and encouragement
- foster familiarity between the child and a sympathetic teaching assistant on a one-to-one basis, in a quiet place, for a short time every day
- try to avoid settings and situations that may cause anxiety
- establish a safe place in the classroom where the child can go when they feel anxious
- create familiar and enjoyable routines and encourage the child to take part
- encourage the child to take part in non-verbal activities, such as games using picture cards, with a familiar adult and perhaps one other child
- encourage verbal or at least gestural responses in safe situations
- make a fun game of cumulatively copying actions, such as nod, stamp, clap, etc., gradually building up until one of you gets it wrong, then maybe add a sound or two
- encourage the child to use visual materials as much as possible to extend learning
- make use of puppets in informal situations where the puppet can do the talking
- encourage creative activities, including art, music, design and technology
- encourage the child to deal with their anxieties when they feel ready to do so.

Support agencies

- Association for all Speech Impaired Children (AFASIC)
- Speech and Language

Semantic pragmatic disorder

Semantic pragmatic disorder is a communication disorder, which crosses the boundaries of both specific language impairment and autistic spectrum disorder. It may be diagnosed as one or other of these conditions or it may be identified specifically.

Children with this disorder are unable to process complex information in social situations. They have difficulties with social relationships and any situation involving communication. They are very inward-looking and are usually unable to empathise or to demonstrate any perceptive responses. They often develop obsessive interests, which they love talking about, but find it difficult to understand that you do not share their enthusiasms. They have the triad of impairments that usually indicate the child is on the autistic spectrum – socialising, language and imagination – and semantic pragmatic disorder is often described as the outer spectrum of autism. Children with this disorder may also have attention deficit disorder or dyslexia.

Key characteristics

A child with semantic pragmatic disorder may

- speak in a grown-up way
- not be able to make eye-contact
- find facial expressions, gestures and body language confusing
- think and speak very literally and in concrete terms
- have difficulty with abstract concepts concerning time (eg. next week) or motivation
- read early or late, but without comprehension
- be either very active or very passive
- be logical and inflexible in following rules and expects everyone else to be the same
- be either a loner or appear over-friendly
- be poor at taking turns or taking part in team games or group activities
- have a dislike of crowds
- have food fads
- find social events challenging, being unsure how to take part or react
- have minor motor-skills problems
- demonstrate over-sensitivity to some everyday noises

- be easily distracted
- suffer from specific language impairment or dyslexia.

Support strategies

You may need to

- give the child practical, hands-on tasks
- provide a quiet, orderly environment
- use visual clues whenever possible
- break instructions into short sentences
- keep to classroom routines as much as possible and help them to cope when change is unavoidable
- avoid abstract concepts whenever possible (the child probably won't understand 'guess' or 'pretend' and will find time words, such as 'long ago', problematical)
- give literal instructions eg. 'put the puzzles in the cupboard' rather than 'tidy away'
- help them to learn strategies for socialising
- provide them with a visual written or pictorial timetable
- explain metaphors, sarcasm and jokes when they are used
- build on their special interests
- follow any given programmes such as from the speech and language therapist
- give constant encouragement and praise.

Support agencies

- Association for all Speech Impaired Children (AFASIC)
- Communications Forum
- I CAN
- National Autistic Society

Specific language impairment

Speech and language impairment can vary a great deal from mild difficulties to severe problems with the understanding and use of language. A specific language impairment is diagnosed when a child has difficulty with language but is developing normally in all other areas. Many children have speech and language difficulties associated with physical, sensory, neurological and intellectual impairment. Over a million children in the UK have some kind of speech and language impairment. One in 500 of these children has an impairment that is both severe and long-term. These children will have difficulties with understanding and using language in one or more areas.

Key characteristics

Children with a specific language impairment may have difficulties with one or more of these areas.

- Phonology – some children have difficulty processing speech sounds and using them correctly, while others confuse or substitute sounds.

- Grammar – some children have difficulty organising words into sentences, using the correct grammatical structure (they often muddle verb tenses and have difficulty with conjunctions and prepositions), or they may have difficulty pronouncing -ed, -ing, and -s endings and sound like much younger children in the way they form their sentences.

- Word finding – some children have difficulty in recalling the right word when they need to use it, having to describe the word rather than naming it eg. 'It's hot. You make tea. You put water in it' for the word 'kettle', which may be caused by their difficulties.

- Semantics (the meanings of words and the way they relate to each other) – this may be affected by poor auditory memory skills and can have serious implications for children in the classroom. If they cannot retain the meaning of new vocabulary, then they will have difficulty understanding new concepts and ideas, which will in turn affect their ability to express their own thoughts.

- Attention and listening – children with attention and listening difficulties have one of two problems. Either they cannot screen out what is unimportant from what they hear and so listen to everything, or they lack skill at controlling attention and therefore miss large chunks of information. Oral whole-class teaching can therefore cause great difficulty for these children.

- Pragmatics (the way that language is used to convey thoughts and feelings) – some children have difficulty in understanding how to use language in different social situations and can make very inappropriate remarks.

Support strategies

You may need to

- use pictures, signs and symbols as teaching aids

- use visual or concrete materials to support the understanding of new conceptual vocabulary across the curriculum

- encourage word association activities to develop word finding skills

- play games to develop an understanding of categories eg. vegetables, fruit, pets

- break instructions into chunks and check for understanding by asking the child to repeat each part

- give opportunities for revision of key concepts and vocabulary

- offer a regular therapy programme to address specific speech and language needs

- use alternative methods of recording eg. mind maps, diagrams, charts, writing frames

- use games to develop listening and attention skills

- use specific ICT programmes eg. *Writing with Symbols*

- use circletime to encourage social interaction and communication skills

- use specific games and activities to develop social communication skills.

Support agencies

- Association for all Speech Impaired Children (AFASIC)

- I CAN

Spina bifida

Spina bifida is one of the most common congenital disabilities, affecting approximately one in 500 births. Improved treatment since the 1980s has meant that more children with spina bifida are surviving. These children are often of average intelligence and need to be able to attend a mainstream school.

Spina bifida is an abnormality of the spinal cord where one or two of the vertebrae do not form properly, thus causing a split, which in turn causes damage to the central nervous system. Most children with spina bifida will need to be in a wheelchair and may need a specially adapted toilet seat or other adaptations.

About 80 per cent of babies born with spina bifida also have hydrocephalus (an accumulation of cerebro-spinal fluid). As with other complex conditions, there are degrees of severity and there are several different types. Spina bifida occulta is a very mild form.

Key characteristics

A child with spina bifida may

- have some incontinence problems in the early years, though these are usually under control by the age of seven
- have weakness or paralysis in the lower limbs and need regular physiotherapy
- have a lack of skin sensation in some parts of their body as a result of nerve damage
- have difficulty sitting still and often appear fidgety and restless

A child with spina bifida who also has hydrocephalus may

- have poor verbal comprehension
- have difficulty understanding some non-verbal cues eg. gestures, tone of voice
- have long-term visual and auditory memory difficulties
- have problems with eye-hand coordination and motor planning
- have great difficulty organising themselves and their belongings
- have some specific learning difficulties
- find it difficult to sustain attention to a task.

Support strategies

You may need to

- have regular meetings with parents and professionals as the child's needs may change over time
- organise physical access to different parts of the school – particularly toilet and washing facilities
- encourage children to take an active part in playground games as there are many games that do not require a high level of running and jumping
- ensure that appropriately trained adult support is provided
- make use of ICT as an aid to learning and encourage the development of word-processing skills
- make use of audio-visual aids
- ensure that extra time is given for specific tasks
- celebrate ability, not disability as some children may be very able in a specific area
- provide clearly structured classroom routines to help the child with developing their own organisational skills
- use pictorial or colour-coded task lists to support independent planning and organisation of tasks
- break instructions into chunks and check for understanding by asking the child to repeat each part
- give opportunities for revision of key concepts and vocabulary
- reinforce new concepts through practical activities related to the child's own experiences
- use circletime to encourage social interaction and communication skills
- use specific games and activities to develop social communication skills.

Support agencies

- Association for Spina Bifida and Hydrocephalus (ASBAH)

Stammering

Stammering, also known as stuttering, is a condition in which the sufferer speaks hesitantly or in a stumbling and jerky way. Stammering varies, both in the way it affects different people and in its severity. A child who stammers may find their fluency varies over time. Stammering can also be episodic. All of this is quite disconcerting for the stammerer, who can never be quite sure how much they will be affected in a given situation.

Children don't usually grow out of stammering completely, but they can learn to manage it, with sensitive encouragement and professional support. The child who stammers will suffer a great deal of anxiety, fear and embarrassment. They need people who are willing to listen patiently and not try to rush them.

As well as the more obvious sufferers, there will be children who seem either shy and reticent to take part in discussions or long-winded in the way they speak, hiding their stammer through pauses, hesitations and rephrasing. It will be hard to detect a stammer in either of these cases.

Strangely enough, many children or adults who stammer noticeably in ordinary conversation appear to be stammer-free when they are able to take on a different role, such as acting or singing.

Key characteristics

The child who stammers may

- prolong spoken sounds eg. 'sssssix'

- repeat particular sounds or beginnings of words eg. 'ta-ta-take'

- have long silences, when they are repeatedly unable to produce the required sound at all

- use hesitations and substitutions, such as 'you know' and 'er', to mask stammering

- play for time by asking the questioner to repeat themselves

- deliberately avoid using particular words or sounds

- demonstrate physical signs of tension eg. blinking, grimacing, sighing, coughing, gulping, swallowing a lot, blushing, avoiding eye-contact

- have low levels of confidence and self-esteem

- avoid responding to questions or participating in discussions whenever possible.

Support strategies

You may need to

- slow down your own rate of speaking so as to reduce the pressure of time

- give the child time to respond – do not interrupt, answer for them or try to finish their sentences

- reduce the number of questions you ask the child who stammers

- encourage them to speak about their own interests as they will probably be able to do this with a greater degree of fluency

- try to find an alternative to the child having to speak in registration sessions

- support them as they learn to read by giving them opportunities to read in unison with another child or alone with an adult where other children cannot hear

- provide the child with a mentor to help alleviate some of their anxieties and frustrations

- create a relaxed and unhurried learning environment

- give lots of encouragement and praise to raise their confidence and self-esteem

- use eye-contact and an interested expression to emphasise your interest in them and in what they say, rather than how they say it

- do not assume a lack of interest in singing or drama, since these may be situations in which the child can leave their stammer behind

- liaise closely with the speech and language therapist.

Support agencies

- The British Stammering Association (BSA)

Tourette syndrome

Tourette syndrome is a hereditary neurological disorder, characterised by repeated involuntary movements or sounds called tics. The symptoms of Tourette syndrome usually appear in the teenage years or earlier and affect about one in 200 people, with three to four times as many boys as girls being affected.

There are two categories of tics. Simple tics are short, sudden, repetitive movements, involving only a few motor or vocal muscles. Complex tics are coordinated patterns of movements involving a larger number of motor or vocal muscles. Tics are irresistible and their severity will come and go from one day to the next. They can be suppressed, but they build up and will reappear with greater frequency and severity once the sufferer relinquishes control. They can become worse if a situation is stressful and improve if a person is relaxed. A number of other disorders are sometimes associated with Tourette syndrome, including attention deficit disorder (ADD), self-harming behaviour and obsessive compulsive disorder, though these are rare.

Most children who have Tourette syndrome suffer with a mild form of the condition, often with transient tics that last for a few weeks or months. However, some children suffer with chronic tics that last for years. The condition can improve late in adolescence.

Children with Tourette syndrome need to be given support to cope with their own frustrations and with the social difficulties which are inevitably associated with this condition.

Key characteristics

Children with Tourette syndrome may

- have facial tics eg. eye-blinking, nose-twitching, sniffing, grimacing, squinting, lip-smacking, tongue-poking
- have other motor tics eg. head-jerking, foot-stamping, body-twisting, neck-stretching, shoulder-shrugging, arm-extending
- have vocal tics eg. throat-clearing, grunting, spitting, swearing, hissing, shouting, barking, moaning, stammering
- have motor control difficulties
- have organisational difficulties

- have low self-esteem
- sometimes suffer from depression and moodiness
- have compulsions or obsessions
- repeat what others say (echolalia)
- shout out obscenities (coprolalia)
- repeat obscene gestures (copropraxia)
- imitate the actions of others (echopraxia)
- be unable to carry out an action (apraxia).

Support strategies

You may need to

- provide opportunities for the child to have short breaks from the classroom
- encourage them to recognise when they need a break
- allow extra time for them to do tasks in order to minimise stress
- develop fine motor skills, using a motor skills programme
- give short, clearly defined tasks
- give opportunities for practical tasks using multisensory strategies
- encourage the child to talk about their difficulties with an adult mentor and to share their concerns with trusted members of their peer group
- allow extra time for taking tests
- teach keyboard skills so that written work can be typed
- break instructions into chunks and check for understanding by asking the child to repeat each part
- use visual and concrete materials to focus attention and aid understanding
- suggest that the child sits in front of the teacher to avoid visual distractions from other children
- suggest that they sit away from windows and other distractions
- look out for signs of depression.

Support agencies

- Tourette Syndrome (UK) Association

Visual impairment

Visual impairment – having little or no sight – has been classified in a number of ways. Health and Social Services use the terms blind for those with very little or no sight and partially sighted for those with a small but useful level of vision.

In education, the terms most commonly used are

- **visually impaired** – this can be a reference to a particular eye problem or to reduced vision resulting from brain damage
- **totally blind** – having no sight at all.

A child is said to be visually impaired if their vision cannot be corrected to within normal limits by any means.

Schools who have visually impaired children will need to make certain adaptations, such as adding white lines at the edges of steps, and to provide specially adapted equipment, such as magnifying screens and large print books. Outreach is usually provided, in the form of specialised advice and support, from a school for blind people or direct from the RNIB.

Key characteristics

A child with visual impairment may

- need the support of the advisory teacher for visually impaired children
- need to use a range of senses to become familiar with the school environment
- have a short attention span
- display unusual fatigue after any kind of visual task
- have poor balance.

A child who has problems with distance vision may

- frown or scowl frequently and have a tendency to blink excessively or rub their eyes
- sit rigidly when reading or viewing a distant object
- turn their head to use one eye only
- lose their place when reading.

A child who has problems with near vision may

- try to avoid close work
- cover or close one eye and hold their head close to the work
- be inattentive when taking part in guided reading
- have awkward head posture generally

- stumble against classroom furniture
- have poor word spacing and be unable to write on a line.

Support strategies

You may need to

- allow more time for hands-on experiences, verbal explanations and completing tasks
- allow more opportunity for work with real objects
- make use of reverse chaining – demonstrating what you want the end result to be like
- provide extra help with organisational skills
- keep the classroom tidy to avoid accidents
- put up bold and accessible wall displays
- verbalise everything that is written on the board
- make sure that the child is sitting in the best place to see your face
- make sure that there is good lighting in the classroom, with no glare
- encourage the child to wear their glasses
- use colour coding to encourage the child to locate or put away equipment
- provide the child with their own books rather than expecting them to share
- encourage independence as much as possible.

Support agencies

- National Federation of Families with Visually Impaired Children (LOOK)
- Royal National Institute for the Blind (RNIB)
- Visual Impairment Centre for Teaching and Research (VICTAR)

Who's who?

A–Z of the various special needs specialist professionals and their roles.

One of the special needs coordinator's responsibilities is to liaise with outside agencies. This glossary outlines the main professionals you are likely to come into contact with and gives brief details of their roles. Of course, there will be differences between education authorities, so you will need to find out exactly how the system works in your own area.

Audiologist

Audiologists are based in hospitals and are qualified in assessing levels of hearing and hearing impairment. They will carry out audiometric tests to measure hearing and give information on hearing impairment. They can give teachers advice and can help to develop classroom ideas for supporting children with hearing loss. They will also advise on aids to improve hearing. In most areas, they make regular visits to the child in school.

Behaviour support teacher

Behaviour support teachers are employed by the LEA and are part of a behaviour support service. They will help the school to establish and maintain an effective whole-school behaviour policy. They often work with individuals or groups of children with emotional and behavioural difficulties within school. They can also run training sessions for teachers, teaching assistants and parents on any aspect of school and home life to do with emotional and behavioural issues.

Carer

This is a person who cares for a child for whom the social services have parental responsibility. The carer, as well as social services, needs to be notified if the school is concerned about a child's educational progress. The carer will have a role to play when considering a child's special educational needs.

Casework officer

This is the person within the LEA who coordinates assessments and provision, and prepares statements of special educational needs. When a request for the formal assessment of a child is received by the LEA, the casework officer coordinates the process.

A statutory assessment involves requesting written reports from a range of professionals who have contact with the child as well as requesting information from parents or carers and the school.

Child and Adult Mental Health Unit

The Child and Adult Mental Health Unit is concerned with various aspects of mental health. It is a special unit, usually attached to a hospital, possibly within a Children's Centre, a Family Centre or a Child Guidance Centre. Clinical psychologists are available to work with children and their families, either at the unit or by making home or school visits. Either the family's GP or the school, or occasionally the social worker or educational welfare officer may refer a child to this service.

Child Guidance Centre

This is sometimes called the Child and Family Centre or the Child and Family Therapeutic Service. This is primarily a centre where children with emotional, behavioural and mental health problems receive assessment and support from a multidisciplinary team of professionals called the child guidance team. These professionals may include a child psychiatrist, a social worker, an educational psychologist, a clinical psychologist and a psychotherapist. The Child Guidance Centre is usually run by the LEA and the local health authority, though it is sometimes run by voluntary organisations. Referrals are usually made through a GP, health visitor, educational psychologist or social worker. *See also* Child and Adult Mental Health Unit.

Childminder

Childminders have to be approved and registered by social services. New childminders seeking registration now have to undergo a period of training approved by the Office for Standards in Education (Ofsted). They are self-employed and work in their own homes looking after an agreed number of children. Arrangements are usually made privately with the parents but, in some circumstances, social services may provide support and circulate a list of approved childminders to those seeking placements for their children. Some childminders have a particular interest in working with children with disabilities and they undertake specific training for that purpose.

Child protection officer/coordinator

All schools must have a child protection officer or coordinator and a back-up child protection officer or coordinator. These roles are often filled by the headteacher and the deputy headteacher, as the responsibility for referral to social services is usually the responsibility of the headteacher. If a referral needs to be made, parents should be informed, unless this would place the child at risk or affect an investigation, for example by alerting an abuser. The child protection officer or coordinator needs to provide information for a referral and a possible case conference. This may include

- factual information about the child, such as date of birth, address and names of parents or carers and other household members, including non-family

- key agencies working with the family

- reasons for referral.

If a child is placed on the child protection register, then the school becomes part of the core group which must ensure that the child protection plan is implemented.

Child psychiatrist

Child psychiatrists are doctors who specialise in childhood mental disorders and related problems. They are employed by the NHS and work with children who have social, emotional, mental or behavioural difficulties. They are involved in diagnosing conditions and recommending treatments.

Clinical psychologist

Clinical psychologists have trained to develop an understanding of how people's minds, abilities and behaviours develop. They are usually employed by the health authority and may work alone or as part of the child guidance team. They can help schools by observing and assessing children with emotional and behavioural difficulties, diagnosing conditions such as autistic spectrum disorder and giving suggestions for managing behaviour within school. They also work together with the child and family to help with any developmental, emotional and behavioural problems. A referral is usually only made directly to a clinical psychologist by a child's GP. A school will need to discuss with the educational psychologist first any child they feel might benefit from working with the clinical psychologist.

Child psychotherapist

Child psychotherapists tend to work with the most disturbed children. They do not need to have been a trained teacher, but have undergone at least four years' specialist training, have a relevant degree and have worked with children. Child psychotherapists often work as part of the child guidance team. They help children to understand their feelings and to deal with their anger or pain.

Community paediatrician

Community paediatricians are based in hospitals or community care trusts and are employed by the NHS. They are qualified doctors, usually consultants, who have specialised in paediatrics (child medicine). GPs and health visitors will refer pre-school children who have physical or medical difficulties to a paediatrician for general assessment. The community paediatrician will then refer the child on to other expert professionals and monitor overall progress. All the professionals involved with the child will be asked for a report if a child is being assessed for a statement of special educational needs. School nurses can also make referrals to a community paediatrician, once the child is of statutory school age.

Educational psychologist

Educational psychologists are qualified teachers who have taught in schools and have then gone on to undertake further training in psychology. They are trained to help children and young people (from birth to 19 years) who are experiencing difficulties in learning or behaviour. Educational psychologists are the professionals who are most likely to work closely with schools, and the special needs coordinator in particular. They may be based in a Child Guidance Centre and will be responsible for several schools – primary, secondary and special. The Educational Psychology Service has to ration numbers of visits to each school per year. In most local authorities the special needs coordinator needs to obtain written consent from the parent or carer before the child is seen by an educational psychologist, although if you have a general query and do not use the child's full name you can discuss any pupil with them.

Educational psychologists are concerned with children's learning and development and their barriers to learning. They are involved in statutory assessment and early identification of learning difficulties and emotional and behavioural difficulties, but their role can be far wider than this.

Their duties will include

- consultations with class teachers for advice about children in general terms
- discussion with the special needs coordinator about particular children who have already been referred to the Educational Psychology Service
- observation, assessment and reporting on children with learning or emotional and behavioural difficulties who have been referred to them
- attending annual reviews of statement meetings for children with statements of special educational needs
- providing INSET for staff on any aspect of their work
- meeting and advising the parents of children with special educational needs
- debriefing staff who have been in a difficult situation with children or parents (this may sometimes include counselling after a bereavement in the school)
- attending liaison meetings in school with other professionals eg. the school nurse or the educational welfare officer
- planning how to reintegrate a child who has been absent for a long time, for example due to ill-health or an accident
- drawing up learning programmes for children or groups of children with special educational needs of various kinds
- introducing circle of friends as a strategy to support a particular child.

Educational welfare officer

Educational welfare officers are employed by the LEA. They will spend time in school on a regular basis monitoring attendance by checking registers, but they have other roles too. Their main responsibilities are

- ensuring children attend school regularly – you can report any child about whose attendance you have concerns to the education welfare officer to follow up including a child who is persistently late or whose parents regularly collect them late
- making home visits – where there are concerns about attendance or to support parents in other appropriate ways
- advising parents of their rights in relation to educational matters
- working with children – counselling on bullying, stealing, truancy, school phobia and any other issues which may affect a child's attendance at school

- involvement with social services, working jointly on some cases
- close liaison with other agencies, often attending liaison meetings along with the educational psychologist, school nurse, special needs coordinator and headteacher
- transport issues
- holiday schemes.

The school can refer a child to the educational welfare officer through the LEA's usual referral channels, or direct on a separate referral form. Also, the officer may identify a child who has poor attendance at school to follow up on.

Family Centre

These are sometimes called Parents' Centres. They are places usually set up and run by parents of children with special needs to offer advice to other parents. The Family Centre will often provide support with the assessment process, tribunals and other matters. They may offer a buddy system where a volunteer will attend meetings at school with parents. This might include being the independent parental supporter when a child is undergoing statutory assessment. Family Centres usually offer

- counselling
- training
- information sessions on various conditions affecting children with special educational needs
- therapy
- advice and guidance for parents.

Family support worker

Family support workers work alongside social workers. They provide a service to children with learning difficulties and disabilities and their families. The family support worker endeavours to be a link between parents and other agencies and often helps parents by putting them in touch with charities, local support groups and other useful organisations.

Health visitor

Health visitors are registered nurses who have undergone further specialist training. They have special responsibility for all children under five and will give new parents a Personal Child Health Record book for their child. Each child has a named health visitor. This health visitor is responsible for carrying out the child's developmental checks. These currently take place at six weeks, six to nine months and pre-school. They include hearing and vision screening, as well as noting the development of speech and language.

At school age, responsibility passes to the school nurse, although health visitors can continue to visit and offer support until a child is 18 years of age if they have special needs.

Health visitors

- visit all homes where there are children under five
- help parents learn to care for their children
- carry out health and developmental checks at regular intervals
- identify and refer children where special needs are suspected
- provide support for parents
- counsel parents
- act as a friend, helping parents to understand what is going on when a child has special needs, explaining all stages of the process and what education and health services can do
- liaise with social workers, nursery staff, etc., where a child has special needs
- build up a relationship with a family from when a child is ten days old, thus often being the first to notice when something is wrong, either through neglect or abuse or because of special needs.

Home tuition service

This service is financed by the LEA to provide tuition for children who are unable to attend school for any reason eg. prolonged illness, recuperation from an accident, permanent exclusion, school phobia. A tutor will be appointed to visit and educate the child at home for a set number of hours each week. *See also* Peripatetic teacher/tutor.

Independent parental supporter (formerly named person)

This can be a relative, a friend or a member of a voluntary support group willing to offer parents advice on special needs, or may be specially trained and nominated by the parent partnership service to provide information, advice and support for the parents of special needs children. They are independent of the local authority and can offer help to parents whose children are being assessed for a statement of educational needs. They may help parents with writing their comments, understanding reports, writing letters and attending meetings. The LEA should identify the independent parental supporter when sending the parents a final copy of the statement. *See also* Parent partnership service.

Learning mentor

A learning mentor is an adult who works with a specific child on a one-to-one basis and offers personal support. They may work with a child who has learning difficulties or a child with high ability.

Learning support assistant (LSA)

This term is widely used for teaching assistants (TAs) who work in classrooms with teachers supporting children with special needs. They may work with an individual child or with groups of children. Usually they support children with the development of basic skills in literacy and numeracy, but in some schools they may be given a much wider brief. They may not have undertaken any formal training. Some LSAs may have started as classroom assistants, helping the teacher with ancillary tasks, and have found their role changing with the growing emphasis on the inclusion of children with special needs. Training is becoming increasingly common, provided by either the LEA or the DfES. *See also* Teaching assistant.

Learning support service

The learning support service is usually provided by the LEA and is composed of specialist teachers who visit schools to advise on support strategies for children with learning difficulties and who may also work with individual children.

Learning support teacher

Learning support teachers usually have additional qualifications in teaching pupils with specific learning difficulties like dyslexia. They may also be qualified to deal with a range of other specific learning difficulties. They may be employed by the LEA, by a group of schools or by one school. They may be peripatetic or school-based. They assess children referred to them by the school and they teach individuals or small groups of children on a regular basis. They support and advise the class teacher, special needs coordinator and parents on a range of teaching and learning issues related to individual children. They may also provide staff training on aspects of special needs in which they have particular expertise.

Multidisciplinary team

In education, the multidisciplinary team is a group made up of several specialists who assess children's difficulties. The team may include a paediatrician, an educational psychologist, a speech and language therapist, an occupational therapist, a social worker and other relevant professionals.

Named LEA officer

The named officer or case worker is an officer of the local education authority who keeps parents informed throughout the process of statutory assessment for a statement of special educational needs. They will explain all the procedures. There is often more than one named officer working for an LEA, usually designated either by the age of the children each works with (under-fives, primary or secondary) or by their geographical area.

Occupational therapist

Occupational therapists help

- children with special educational needs

- elderly people who need help to function at home

- anyone who has a temporary disability due to accident, illness or medical treatment which has led to loss of function

- anyone who has a disability and who needs help to gain maximum independent function.

Occupational therapists work with children in a variety of settings, such as

- specialist departments in or affiliated to general hospitals

- children's hospitals

- psychiatric hospitals

- schools

- residential care settings

- the child's own home.

Occupational therapists are employed by

- health trusts

- social services departments

- some independent special schools

- independent and voluntary organisations.

Children can be referred to an occupational therapist through the local social services department or their family doctor. Occupational therapists work with children who have

- physical disabilities as a result of cerebral palsy, spina bifida, head injuries, neurological disorders and other conditions

- limb deficiencies as a result of congenital problems or traumatic amputations

- learning disabilities

- developmental coordination disorder as a result of dyspraxia (children often described as clumsy)

- perceptual difficulties including visual impairment, visual memory and visual-spatial relationship problems

- emotional and behavioural problems

- other medical or traumatic difficulties such as cancer or severe burns.

As well as working in different settings, occupational therapists also work in a variety of different ways. These include

- individual sessions – for such areas as life skills, seating assessment and adaptation, assessment and modification of computer access

- small groups – for developing social skills, life skills and play

- classroom activities – for helping to devise and implement handwriting programmes

- ensuring the effectiveness of seating adaptations in the classroom setting

- advising on and providing a range of equipment or adaptations for schools, especially designed for use by or with disabled children eg. splints, standing frames, wheelchair trays, adjustable tables, bookstands, toilet adaptations, hoists

- working through people – training parents and others, including teachers and support staff.

Opportunity group leader

Opportunity groups are pre-school settings which are set up in most areas to provide appropriate support for children with special needs or with difficult home circumstances. Opportunity groups, however, are not exclusively for special needs children – their aim is to include the full range of pre-school children. The opportunity group leader is the person with whom you, as special needs coordinator, will liaise regarding children due to attend your school.

Parent partnership service

This is a service set up by or with the support of the LEA, but which must be independent from it, to provide parents with information, advice and support. This is the service which trains and provides the independent parental supporter, whose details are given to parents when their child is the subject of a statutory assessment. Schools should liaise with this service so that parents can be put in touch with their local independent parental supporter whenever they want help or support. See also Independent parental supporter.

Peripatetic teacher/tutor

Peripatetic teachers and tutors are usually employed by the LEA. They visit schools and help individual children, usually those with statements. They provide specialist support to help meet the targets on the child's statement and/or IEP. Peripatetic teachers also teach children at home if they are unable to attend school for a long period of time due to ill-health. Support assistants can also work on a peripatetic basis.

Physiotherapist

Children's physiotherapists are state registered and are usually employed by the NHS via health trusts. Many, though, are employed direct by schools, particularly non-maintained special schools. They can work with children from birth to the age at which they leave school. They work in a great variety of different locations such as

- hospital maternity wards and special care baby units
- hospital children's wards and outpatient clinics
- specialist children's hospitals
- child development centres
- local health centres
- schools – including special schools or units, mainstream nurseries and schools, residential schools and independent schools
- children's own homes.

There is a wide range of children's conditions that may need physiotherapy, including

- respiratory conditions at birth in pre-term and term babies
- respiratory conditions such as cystic fibrosis in infants and children
- neurological conditions such as cerebral palsy, hydrocephalus and head injuries
- syndromes affecting development
- developmental delay/visual and hearing impairment
- learning disabilities
- coordination problems such as dyspraxia
- chronic conditions affecting the joints, such as juvenile idiopathic or rheumatoid arthritis
- progressive illnesses such as muscular dystrophy
- terminal and non-terminal illnesses such as cancer
- injuries such as burns

- congenital skeletal conditions
- limb deficiencies
- orthopaedic problems including post-operative trauma.

What a physiotherapist actually provides will depend on the particular needs of individual children but it is likely to include such things as

- hands-on treatment on a regular basis
- programmes of exercise which can be implemented by parents, teaching assistants or others
- programmes of movement to prevent the development of deformity and maintain a range of movement and functional ability
- the identification, supply and monitoring of appliances, aids, seating, standing frames, wheelchairs and so on, usually in conjunction with the occupational therapist
- advice to nurseries and schools concerning access to the environment, mobility, special seating or equipment, the use of splints, access to physical education, and ways of involving the child or adapting activities to allow him or her to achieve success in practical subjects
- encouragement towards maximum independence
- referral to other health care professionals such as the occupational therapist or speech and language therapist
- written advice for any statutory assessment of special educational needs
- written reports for, and attendance at, reviews.

Physiotherapists work with children in the most appropriate way. This might be

- individual sessions – particularly for post-trauma or post-operation rehabilitation, chest conditions, developmental or neurological problems
- group sessions – particularly for coordination problems such as dyspraxia
- through others – such as parents and learning support staff in schools.

Play therapist

The play therapist may work in a child guidance centre or hospital. They help children to explore their feelings and face difficult situations through play. A therapist may guide the child's play or observe them playing.

Portage

Portage is the pre-school support system for children with severe special needs or whose development has been significantly delayed. The portage worker, usually employed by the local authority, is the link person between parents and all the professionals involved in supporting their child. The portage worker will make home visits to advise and support the parents as well as to devise a programme of play-based activities the parents can do with their child at home. When the child is about to start school, the portage worker will liaise with the school in order to ensure a smooth transition.

Responsible person

The governors of the school must designate a responsible person, who is usually the headteacher, or possibly the special needs coordinator or the special needs governor. The responsible person must be informed by the LEA when a pupil at that school is provided with a statement of special educational needs. It is then the duty of the responsible person to ensure that all members of staff who may teach or support that child know that they have a statement of special educational needs, what it is for and what targets are set within it.

School doctor

The work of the school doctor is closely related to the community paediatrician's role, except that in some areas the school doctor is exclusively employed to visit schools and assess children's needs. They can make recommendations, assess specific conditions and review individual cases over time. Children will usually be referred to the school doctor through the educational psychologist or the school nurse. The special needs caseworker may also ask the school doctor to assess the child as part of the statutory assessment process, towards the provision of a statement of special educational needs.

School nurse

School nurses are trained nurses employed by the health service. They take over responsibility for children from the health visitor once they reach statutory school age. School nurses carry out developmental checks, including hearing and vision, usually in Year 1 and Year 4. However, the school can ask a school nurse to visit at any time, with parental consent or at parents' behest, to carry out checks on children. These checks could concern sight, hearing, weight, height or general health issues.

School nurses work with other professionals. They are part of the child health team, which also includes health visitors, community paediatricians and GPs. They have access to all medical records on the child.

Special needs adviser

The special needs adviser is a member of the advice and development team for your LEA. They can offer support and encouragement to special needs coordinators, especially those who are new to the role. They will run courses, answer telephone queries and, depending on your local authority, visit you in school to give support. They have a responsibility to monitor SEN provision in schools across the LEA.

Special needs coordinator (SENCo)

The special needs coordinator is the teacher with overall responsibility for coordinating provision for children with special educational needs in the school and for monitoring their progress. The 2001 SEN Code of Practice outlines the role and responsibilities of the special needs coordinator, including

- 'overseeing the day to day operation of the school's SEN policy
- coordinating provision for children with special educational needs
- liaising with and advising fellow teachers
- managing learning support assistants
- overseeing the records of all children with special educational needs
- liaising with parents of children with special educational needs
- contributing to the in-service training of staff
- liaising with external agencies including the LEA's support and educational psychology services, health and social services, and voluntary bodies.' (DfES, 2001, para 5:32)

Special needs governor

Governing bodies are required to nominate one of their members to have special responsibility for special needs. They may or may not have any expertise or experience in the area. All governors are volunteers, and most are lay people with an interest in, but not necessarily an inside knowledge of, education. The special needs governor is no different. Together with the special needs coordinator, they are responsible for reporting to parents on the implementation of the school's special needs policy and they should meet with the special needs coordinator on a regular basis. In a few schools, this role may be taken by a special committee.

Special needs panel

This is the group responsible for making decisions about statutory assessment within the LEA. It usually consists of one of a named officer, an educational psychologist or a special needs adviser plus other professionals. Requests for statements and funding for specialist equipment are submitted to this group. How often they meet will vary from one authority to another – sometimes it is as often as fortnightly.

Social worker

Social workers are employed by the social services department of the local authority. They have responsibility for child protection issues, children in need and looked after children. Social workers are responsible for maintaining a register of children considered to be at risk.

There are eight categories in which children in need may meet the criteria.

1 Abuse or neglect.

2 Significant disability or intrinsic condition. Most of these will be children with medically diagnosed conditions such as cerebral palsy, autism or Down syndrome. In these cases, there will be a greater need for support than is available through the main carers.

3 Parental illness or disability.

4 Family in acute stress. This includes families who normally function adequately but whose daily life has been disrupted by circumstances such as unemployment, homelessness or a death in the family.

5 Family dysfunction. In this case parenting is always inadequate.

6 Socially unacceptable behaviour. These are children who have a detrimental effect on the community.

7 Low income. These families will have an income below the standard state entitlement, but are not those families who are unable to manage on the entitlement.

8 Absent parent. This includes children whose parents have died, or are in prison.

Looked after children are those who are subject to a care order. These children may be living with their families with social work support or living in foster placements or in residential provision.

There are a variety of reasons for children being looked after, including

- risk of harm and the need to be moved to a safer place

- a parent being unable to continue caring for them

- a parent being ill or needing to go into hospital with no other family available to care for the child.

Social services now need to ensure that every child and young person in public care has a personal education plan (PEP). The plan ensures access to services and support, contributes to stability, minimises disruption and broken schooling, signals particular and special needs, establishes clear goals and acts as a record of progress and achievement.

When a child enters public care their social worker should inform both the school and the LEA. The social worker is responsible for initiating the personal education plan. This should be done in partnership with the child, the designated teacher, the parent or relevant family member, the carer and any other person who may have relevant involvement with the child. This may be a health professional or an educational psychologist if there are assessments taking place in either of these areas.

Speech and language therapist

Speech and language therapy, in most cases, is considered to be an educational provision and is usually funded jointly by the LEA and the NHS health trust. There is a distinction between educational needs and non-educational needs. This means that if a child has a medical need that doesn't have a direct effect on their learning then that need is regarded as non-educational, and is to be met with non-educational provision.

Speech and language therapists offer their services in a variety of venues, including

- clinics

- hospitals

- community health centres

- day nurseries

- opportunity play groups

- mainstream schools

- special language units attached to mainstream schools

- colleges.

Although many parents often ask for referrals to a speech and language therapist via their GP this is not strictly necessary. Parents can refer their child directly to a speech and language therapist themselves. Details of the service can be obtained from the local NHS trust. Some children who require long-term speech and language therapy may be considered for a statement of educational needs. Children with severe difficulties may need specialist help during the whole of their school life and into adulthood.

Most speech and language therapists working with school-age children are expected to

- work collaboratively with parents and staff within a mainstream educational setting

- take account of the family and educational context in order to inform assessment, diagnosis and therapy

- provide education and training for both parents and school staff in all aspects of language and communication difficulties

- support teachers with suggested strategies for teaching children with language and communication difficulties across the curriculum

- liaise with other professionals – such as educational psychologists and specialist teachers – who may have been involved with the child.

Speech and language therapists may assess a child as having a receptive language impairment (difficulty in understanding language) or an expressive language impairment (difficulty in using language). Some children may be diagnosed as having both receptive and expressive language impairments. Speech and language therapists are concerned with a range of communication problems including

- language delay – arising from a range of sources including poor language environment

- phonology – speech sound development

- prosody – the way that we speak, using intonation and stress

- dysfluency – stammering

- articulation – the production of meaningful speech sounds by the coordinated movements of the lips, tongue, jaw, teeth and palate

- syntax or grammar – the way that words and parts of words are used together in phrases and sentences

- semantics – understanding the meaning of words, phrases and sentences

- pragmatics – understanding how feelings are conveyed through language and how language is used in different social situations.

Speech and language therapists work with children in different ways. These include

- individual withdrawal sessions

- small group withdrawal sessions

- class-based individual or small group sessions

- through other people.

Often a speech and language therapist will work through other people. This means that someone else – usually a teaching assistant – implements part of an agreed therapy plan devised by or in conjunction with a therapist. This can be very efficient and effective but demands a high level of training and understanding by those delivering such sessions.

Teaching assistant

The member of staff who is likely to be most involved on a day-to-day basis with supporting individuals or groups of children in classrooms. They are often known as learning support assistants if their role is specifically that of supporting the learning of children with special educational needs. See also Learning support assistant.

Special needs support groups

A–Z of voluntary organisations, agencies and support groups.

The following list includes the main agencies for each type of condition, plus some general advice and counselling services for parents and teachers. It is arranged in alphabetical order by group name.

Organisation	Description	Contact details
ABC for Reading	A national charity to support those with Irlen syndrome. This is a visual perception difficulty where sensitivity to light can cause problems with print on a page.	4 Park Farm Business Centre, Fornham St Genevieve, Bury St Edmunds, Suffolk IP28 6TS Tel: 01284 724301
ACE Centre (Aiding Communication in Education)	A centre giving advice and supplying software for young people with communication and physical difficulties.	92 Windmill Road. Headington, Oxford OX3 7DR Tel: 01865 759800 www.ace-centre.org.uk
Action for ME (AfME)	A voluntary support group providing information, advice and support for ME sufferers and their families.	PO Box 1302, Wells, Somerset BA5 1YE Tel: 01749 670799 www.afme.org.uk
Action for Sick Children	Advice and support.	c/o The National Children's Bureau, 8 Wakley Street, London EC1V 7QE Tel: 020 7843 6444
ADD/ADHD Family Support Group UK	Information and support to parents and professionals, related to attention deficit/hyperactivity disorder.	1a High Street, Dilton Marsh, Westbury, Wiltshire BA13 4DL Tel: 01373 826045 www.addcontact.org.uk
ADD Information Services (ADDISS)	Information and support related to attention deficit disorder for parents, teachers and healthcare workers.	PO Box 340, Edgware, Middlesex HA8 9HL Tel: 020 8906 9068 www.addiss.co.uk
ADDNET UK	National website for attention deficit/hyperactivity disorder.	Tel: 020 8260 1400 or 020 8516 1413 www.btinternet.com/~black.ice/addnet
Advisory Centre for Education (ACE)	An independent national advice centre for parents. Provides advice on all aspects of education, including SEN.	Unit 1C, Aberdeen Studios, 22 Highbury Grove, London N5 2DQ Advice line: 0808 800 5793 (Mon–Fri 2–5pm) www.ace-ed.org.uk
AFASIC (Association for all Speech Impaired Children)	A national organisation that provides information and support about speech and language disorders.	50–52 Great Sutton Street, London EC1V 0DJ Helpline: 0845 355 5577 www.afasic.org.uk
Allergy UK	Advice and support for people with allergies.	Deepdene House, 30 Bellegrove Road, Welling, Kent DA16 5PY Helpline: 020 8303 8583 (Mon–Fri 9am–9pm, Sat 10am–1pm) www.allergyfoundation.com
Alliance for Inclusive Education (ALLFIE)	Supports inclusive education for all children.	Unit 2, 70 South Lambeth Road, London SW8 1RL Tel: 020 7735 5277 www.allfie.org.uk
Anaphylaxis Campaign	Gives information for those who have a severe allergy to nuts or other foods, insect stings, rubber, or anything else.	PO Box 275, Farnborough, Hampshire GU14 6SX Tel: 01252 542029 www.anaphylaxis.org.uk
Arthritis Care	Voluntary organisation working with and for all people with arthritis.	18 Stephenson Way, London NW1 2HD Tel: 020 7380 6500 www.arthritiscare.org.uk

Organisation	Description	Contact details
Association for Brain Damaged Children and Young Adults	Information and support.	Clifton House, 3 St Paul's Road, Coleshill, Coventry CV56 5DE Tel: 024 7666 5450
Association for Children with Heart Disorders	Support organisation to share contacts, information, experiences, support and help.	26 Elizabeth Drive, Helmshore, Rossendale, Lancashire BB4 4JB Tel: 01706 213632 www.tachd.org.uk or www.heartchild.info
Association for Children with Life Threatening or Terminal Conditions (ACT)	Provides information on support services available for families.	Orchard House, Orchard Lane, Bristol BS1 5DT Tel: 0117 922 1556 www.act.org.uk
Association for Restricted Growth	Information and support.	103 St Thomas Avenue, Hayling Island, Hampshire PO11 0EU Tel: 01707 461813
Association for Spina Bifida and Hydrocephalus (ASBAH)	Provides information, support and publications for people with spina bifida and hydrocephalus. It also provides information and support for carers.	ASBAH House, 42 Park Road, Peterborough, Cambridgeshire PE1 2UQ Tel: 01733 555988 www.asbah.org
Association of Workers for Children with Emotional and Behavioural Difficulties (AWCEBD)	Supports those who work with children and young people who have emotional and behavioural difficulties.	Charlton Court, East Sutton, Maidstone, Kent ME17 3DG Tel: 01622 843104 www.awcebd.co.uk
Association of Young People with ME (AYME)	Help, support and contacts for children and young people with ME.	PO Box 605, Milton Keynes MK2 2XD Tel: 01908 373300 www.ayme.org.uk
Asthma and Allergy Information and Research (AAIR)	Education and research into asthma and other allergic diseases.	c/o 12 Vernon Street, Derby DE1 1FT www.users.globalnet.co.uk/~aair
Ataxia UK (formerly the **Friedrich's Ataxia Group**)	Information and support.	10 Winchester House, Kennington Park, Cranmer Road, London SW9 6EJ Helpline: 020 7820 3900 www.ataxia.org.uk
Autism Independent UK (formerly **SFTAH**)	Raising awareness of autism in the UK	199–205 Blandford Avenue, Kettering, Northants NN16 9AT Tel: 01536 523274 www.autismuk.com
Brain and Spine Foundation	Helpline service for people with neurological conditions and their families.	7 Winchester House, Cranmer Road, London SW9 6EJ Tel: 0808 808 1000 www.bbsf.org.uk
British Association of Teachers of the Deaf (BATOD)	Organises meetings and publishes a journal relating to the education of hearing impaired children.	21 The Haystacks, High Wycombe, Buckinghamshire HP13 6PY Tel: 01494 464190 www.batod.org.uk
British Deaf Association	Information, advice and publications related to hearing impairment.	1–3 Worship Street, London EC2A 2AB Tel: 020 7588 3520 www.britishdeafassociation.org.uk
British Dyslexia Association (BDA)	Provides advice, support and information on dyslexia.	98 London Road, Reading, Berkshire RG1 5AU Helpline: 0118 966 8271 www.bda-dyslexia.org.uk
British Dyslexics	Organisation that provides free information, advice, assessment and support to parents of children with dyslexia.	22 Deeside Enterprise Centre, Deeside, Chester CH5 1PP Info line: 01352 716656 Tel: 01244 822884 or 01244 815552 www.dyslexia.uk.com
British Epilepsy Association (also known as **Epilepsy Action**)	Raises awareness of epilepsy and provides information, advice and support for sufferers and their families.	New Anstey House, Gate Way Drive, Yeadon, Leeds LS19 7NW Tel: 0113 210 8800 www.epilepsy.org.uk
British Institute for Brain Injured Children (BIBIC)	Provides therapy to help rehabilitate children who have been diagnosed with a range of conditions.	Knowle Hall, Knowle, Bridgwater, Somerset TA7 8PJ Tel: 01278 684060 www.bibic.org.uk

Organisation	Description	Contact details
British Institute of Learning Disabilities (BILD)	BILD provide services that promote good practice in the provision and planning of health and social care services for people with learning disabilities.	Campion House, Green Street, Kidderminster, Worcestershire DY10 1JL Tel: 01562 723010 www.bild.org.uk
British Heart Foundation	Information and advice for sufferers, parents and teachers plus news of events and research.	14 Fitzhardinge Street, London W1H 6DH Tel: 020 7935 0185 www.bhf.org.uk
British Stammering Association (BSA)	Supports research into stammering, promotes effective therapies and offers support to those who are affected by stammering.	15 Old Ford Road, London E2 9PJ Tel: 020 8983 1003 www.stammering.org
Brittle Bone Society	A national charity that provides a helpline and supports people who have brittle bone disease and their families.	30 Guthrie Street, Dundee DD1 5BS Helpline: 0800 028 2459 www.brittlebone.org
Cancer and Leukaemia in Childhood Trust (CLIC)	Provides care and support for children with cancer and leukaemia and help for their families.	Abbey Wood, Bristol BS34 7JU Tel: 0117 311 2600 www.clic.uk.com
Capability Scotland	Advice and support for adults and children with special needs, but particularly cerebral palsy.	11 Ellersly Road, Edinburgh EH12 6HY Tel: 0131 313 5510 www.capability-scotland.org.uk
Careline	A counselling service for those with anxieties relating to any issue, including special educational needs.	Cardinal Heenan Centre, 326 High Road, Ilford, Essex IG1 1QP Tel: 020 8514 1177
Cerebra (formerly the Rescue Foundation for the Brain Injured Infant)	Information about and support for cerebral palsy, hydrocephalus, ADD, aphasia and learning disabilities.	Principality Buildings, 13 Guildhall Square, Carmarthen, Carmarthenshire SA31 1PR Tel: 01267 244200 or 0800 328 1159 www.cerebra.org.uk
Childline	Free helpline for children needing support with anxieties and fears regarding bullying, abuse and any other problems.	Studd Street, London N1 0QW Children's helpline: 0800 1111 www.childline.org.uk
Children's Chronic Arthritis Association (CCAA)	Information, advice and support.	Ground Floor, Amber Gate, City Wall Road, Worcester WR1 2AH Tel: 01905 745595 www.ccaa.org.uk
Children's Heart Federation	Provides information sheets, support and contact to all families of children with heart disorders.	52 Kennington Oval, London SE11 5SW Tel: 0808 808 5000 www.childrens-heart-fed.org.uk
Children's Liver Disease Foundation	Cares for all families and children with liver disease and provides research, education and support.	36 Great Charles Street, Birmingham B3 3JY Tel: 0121 212 3829 www.childliverdisease.org
Children's Society	Helps children who face problems and their families through residential projects, events, outings and challenges.	Edward Rudolf House, Margery Street, London WC1X 0JL Tel: 0845 300 1128 www.the-childrens-society.org.uk
Children with AIDS Charity (CWAC)	Gives support to children with AIDS and their families. Helps them to live as normal a life as possible. Can provide financial assistance.	Lion House, 3 Plough Yard, London EC2A 3LP Tel: 020 7247 9115 www.cwac.org
Children with Diabetes	Website which aims to develop contacts for parents and children who live with diabetes.	www.childrenwithdiabetes.co.uk
Children with Leukaemia Trust (CWLT)	Information and contacts on leukaemia plus news and events.	London House, 100 New King's Road, London SW6 4LX Tel: 020 7731 8199 www.leukaemia.org.uk
Clear Vision Project (materials for visually impaired children)	Nationwide postal lending library of children's picture books in print and Braille (ideal for sighted and Braille readers together) and books with tactile features for Key Stages 1 and 2.	Linden Lodge School, 61 Princes Way, London SW19 6JB Tel: 020 8789 9575 www.clearvisionproject.org
Cleft Lip and Palate Association (CLAPA)	Offers information and support to sufferers of cleft lip or palate and their families.	Third Floor, 235–237 Finchley Road, London NW3 6LS Tel: 020 7431 0033 www.clapa.com

Organisation	Description	Contact details
CLIMB (Metabolic Diseases in Children)	Provides information, counselling and advice for families and children. Also has grants for equipment, etc.	176 Nantwich Road, Crewe, Cheshire CW2 6BG Tel: 0870 7700 326 www.climb.org.uk
Communications Forum	Information, news and resources for people with communication impairment and their carers.	Tel: 020 7582 9200 www.communicationsforum.co.uk
Contact-a-Family	Support for families of children with special needs. The *Caf Directory* has information about a range of conditions. Puts parents in touch with national networks.	209–211 City Road, London EC1V 1JN Tel: 020 7608 8700 www.cafamily.org.uk
Council for Disabled Children	Information about services and facilities for children with disabilities and special needs.	National Children's Bureau, 8 Wakley Street, London EC1V 7QE Tel: 020 7843 6061 www.ncb.org.uk
Cystic Fibrosis Resource Centre	An online resource centre for sufferers.	www.cysticfibrosis.co.uk
Cystic Fibrosis Trust	Offers support and advice to families and people with cystic fibrosis, also fundraising and public awareness.	11 London Road, Bromley, Kent BR1 1BY Tel: 020 8464 7211 www.cftrust.org.uk
Deaf Education Through Listening and Talking (DELTA)	Information and support on hearing impairment in education.	PO Box 20, Haverhill, Suffolk CB9 7BD Tel: 01440 783689 www.deafeducation.org.uk
DIAL (UK) Disability	Disability information and support lines.	St. Catherine's, Tickhill Road, Doncaster DN4 8QN Tel: 01302 310123 www.dialuk.org.uk
Diabetes UK (formerly the British Diabetic Association)	The charity works for people with diabetes, funding research, campaigning and helping people live with the condition.	10 Parkway, London NW1 7AA Tel: 020 7424 1000 www.diabetes.org.uk
Down Syndrome Education Trust	Interested in the education of children with Down syndrome. Offers advice, support services, publications and workshops for parents.	The Sarah Duffen Centre, Belmont Street, Southsea, Portsmouth, Hampshire PO5 1NA Tel: 023 9285 5330 www.downsed.org
Down's Syndrome Association	Information, advice, publications, counselling and support.	155 Mitcham Road, London SW17 9PG Tel: 020 8682 4001 www.dsa-uk.com
Down's Syndrome Scotland (formerly the Scottish Down's Syndrome Association)	Information, support, publications and educational advice.	158–160 Balgreen Road, Edinburgh EH11 3AU Tel: 0131 313 4225 www.dsscotland.org.uk
Dyscovery Centre	Provides assessment and advice on dyslexia and dyspraxia.	4a Church Road, Whitchurch, Cardiff CF14 2DZ Tel: 029 2062 8222 www.dyscovery.co.uk
Dyslexia in Scotland (formerly the Scottish Dyslexia Association)	Information, advice and support on all aspects of dyslexia.	Stirling Business Centre, Wellgreen, Stirling FK8 2DZ Tel: 01786 446650 www.dyslexia.scotland.dial.pipex.com
Dyslexia Institute	A national dyslexia teaching organisation. It trains specialist teachers to assess and teach people with dyslexia.	133 Gresham Road, Staines, Middlesex TW18 2AJ Tel: 01784 463851 www.dyslexia-inst.org.uk
Dyspraxia Foundation (formerly the Dyspraxia Trust)	Gives advice, support and information on dyspraxia.	8 West Alley, Hitchin, Hertfordshire SG5 1EG Helpline: 01462 454986 www.dyspraxiafoundation.org.uk
English Sports Association for People with Learning Disability (ESAPLD)	Provides opportunities for sport for people who have a learning disability.	Unit 9, Milner Way, Ossett, West Yorkshire WF5 9JN Tel: 01924 267555 www.esapld.co.uk

Organisation	Description	Contact details
Epilepsy Action	Information and support.	New Anstey House, Gate Way Drive, Yeadon, Leeds LS19 7NW Helpline: 0808 800 5050 (Mon–Fri 9am–4.30pm) www.epilepsy.org.uk
Family Fund	Finance for holidays, equipment, etc. for families of children with special needs.	PO Box 50, York YO1 1ZX Tel: 01904 621115 www.familyfundtrust.org.uk
Foundation for People with Learning Disabilities	Works to improve the lives of people with learning disabilities through research, development projects, listening to people with learning disabilities and involving them in work, information and events.	7th Floor, 83 Victoria Steet, London SW1H 0HW Tel: 020 7802 0300 www.learningdisabilities.org.uk
Fragile X Society (UK)	Information and support for parents, produces information booklets and leaflets.	53 Winchelsea Lane, Hastings TN35 4LG Tel: 01424 813147 www.fragilex.org.uk
Friends for the Young Deaf (FYD)	Information and support for hearing impaired children. *See also* National Deaf Children's Society.	120 Abbey Street, Nuneaton CV10 5BY Tel: 024 7635 3766 www.ndcs.org.uk/fyd/
Give Rheumatoid Arthritis Children Encouragement (GRACE)	An organisation run by parents of a child with juvenile chronic arthritis, to give support and information to other parents.	50 Wood Street, St Annes, Lancashire FY8 1QG Helpline: 01253 720303 www.fyldecoast.co.uk/grace/grace.htm
Guillain Barre Syndrome Support Group of the UK	Information and support.	c/o Lincolnshire County Council, Eastgate, Sleaford NG34 7EB Helpline: 0800 374803 www.gbs.org.uk
Haemophilia Society	Advice and information.	Chesterfield House, 385 Euston Road, London NW1 3AU Helpline: 0800 018 6068 www.haemophilia.org.uk
Hearing Research Trust (also known as **Defeating Deafness**)	Information for parents and professionals on all aspects of hearing impairment.	330–332 Gray's Inn Road, London WC1X 8EE Info: 0808 808 2222 www.defeatingdeafness.org
Helen Arkell Dyslexia Centre	Support, information, publications, assessments and training.	Frensham, Farnham, Surrey GU10 3BW Tel: 01252 792400 www.arkellcentre.org.uk
HemiHelp	Provides information and support for children with hemiplegia and their families.	Bedford House, 215 Balham High Road, London SW17 7BQ Helpline: 020 8672 3179 www.hemihelp.org.uk
Huntingdon's Disease Association	Information and support.	108 Battersea High Street, London SW11 3HP Tel: 020 7223 7000 (9am–4.30pm) www.hda.org.uk
Hyperactive Children's Support Group	Support for hyperactive children and their parents.	71 Whyke Lane, Chichester, Sussex PO19 7PD Tel: 01243 551313 www.hacsg.org.uk
I CAN	Advice, support and information for parents of children with speech and communication difficulties. Also gives advice to professionals.	4 Dyer's Buildings, London EC1N 2QP Tel: 0870 010 4066 www.ican.org.uk
IPSEA (The Independent Panel for Special Educational Advice)	Advice to parents from independent experts on all aspects of SEN provision.	6 Carlow Mews, Woodbridge, Suffolk IP12 1DH Advice: 0800 018 4016 Scotland: 0131 454 0082 Northern Ireland: 01232 705654 www.ipsea.org.uk
Irlen Centres UK	Diagnosis and treatment for Irlen syndrome – a visual perception problem.	137 Bishop's Mansions, Stevenage Road, London SW6 6DX Tel: 020 7736 5752 www.irlenuk.com
Kidscape	Information and advice for children. Telephone counselling for parents. Has a preventative policy and prefers to act before bullying or abuse has taken place.	2 Grosvenor Gardens, London SW1W 0DH Tel: 020 7730 3300 www.kidscape.org.uk

Organisation	Description	Contact details
Kids Link	A website which provides information and support for parents of children with special educational needs and links to special needs websites.	http://sargon.mmu.ac.uk
Leukaemia Care Society	Information and support.	2 Shrubbery Avenue, Worcester WR1 1QH Tel: 01905 330003 or 0845 767 3303 www.leukemiacare.org
ME Association	Support, information and advice for ME sufferers.	4 Top Angel, Buckingham Industrial Park, Buckingham MK18 1TH Tel: 0871 781 0008 www.meassociation.org.uk
Mencap	Family support, information and educational advice related to learning disabilities and mental health.	123 Golden Lane, London EC1Y 0RT Tel: 020 7454 0454 www.mencap.org.uk
Mind (The National Association for Mental Health)	Provides advice and information.	15–19 Broadway, Stratford, London E15 4BQ Tel: 020 8519 2122 www.mind.org.uk
Muscular Dystrophy Group (also known as **Muscular Dystrophy Campaign**)	Provides information, counselling, advice and care for those with muscular dystrophy and their families.	7–11 Prescott Place, London SW4 6BS Tel: 020 7720 8055 www.muscular-dystrophy.org
National AIDS Trust (NAT)	Provides information and support services for families and carers.	New City Cloisters, 196 Old Street, London EC1V 9FR Tel: 020 7814 6767 www.nat.org.uk
National Association for Colitis and Crohn's Disease	Advice, information and support for sufferers and their families.	4 Beaumont House, Sutton Road, St Albans Hertfordshire AL1 5HH Tel: 0845 130 2233 www.nacc.org.uk
National Association for Special Educational Needs (NASEN)	Aims to promote the education, training, advancement and development of all those working with children with special educational needs.	NASEN House, 4/5 Amber Business Village, Amber Close, Amington, Tamworth B77 4RP Tel: 01827 311500 www.nasen.org.uk
National Asthma Campaign	UK charity funds research, education and support. Works in partnership with people with asthma and their families.	Providence House, Providence Place, London N1 0NT Helpline: 0845 701 0203 Tel: 020 7226 2260 www.asthma.org.uk
National Autistic Society	Advice, information and support for parents and professionals.	393 City Road, London EC1V 1NG Advice line: 0870 600 8585 www.nas.org.uk
National Autistic Society Scotland	Advice, information and support.	Central Chambers, First Floor, 109 Hope Street, Glasgow G2 6LL Tel: 0141 221 8090 www.nas.org.uk/scotland/index.html
National Autistic Society Wales	Advice, information and support.	William Knox House, Suite C1, Britannic Way, Llandarcy, Neath, West Glamorgan SA10 6EL Tel: 01792 815915
National Children's Bureau	Promotes the interests and well-being of all children and young people across every aspect of their lives.	8 Wakley Street, London EC1B 7QE Tel: 020 7843 6000 www.ncb.org.uk/about.htm
National Deaf Children's Society (NDCS)	Supports and advises hearing impaired children and their families.	15 Dufferin Street, London EC1Y 8UR Tel: 020 7490 8656 Helpline: 0808 800 8880 www.ndcs.org.uk
National Federation of the Blind (UK)	Campaigning for the visually impaired.	Sir John Wilson House, 215 Kirkgate, Wakefield WF1 1JG Tel: 01924 291313 www.nfbuk.org
National Federation of Families with Visually Impaired Children (LOOK)	Information and support.	Queen Alexandra College, 49 Court Oak Road, Harbourne, Birmingham B17 9TG Tel: 0121 428 5038 www.look-uk.org

Organisation	Description	Contact details
National Fragile X Foundation (USA)	Information and research on fragile X syndrome.	PO Box 190488, San Francisco, California 94119 USA Tel: 00 1 800 688 8765 www.fragilex.org
National Meningitis Trust	Information and support.	Fern House, Bath Road, Stroud, Gloucestershire GL5 3TJ 24–hour helpline: 0845 6000 800 www.meningitis-trust.org.uk
National Phobics Society	Support for sufferers of anxiety disorders, including school phobia.	Zion Community Resource Centre, 339 Stretford Road, Hulme, Manchester M15 4ZY Tel: 0870 770 0456 www.phobics-society.org.uk
National Portage Association	Works with the parents of young children with special educational needs.	PO Box 3075, Yeovil BA21 3FB Tel: 01935 471641 www.portage.org.uk
National Pyramid Trust	Advocates and supports low cost, positive intervention for moderate learning difficulties, etc. Helps schools to set up clubs to build self-esteem, confidence and social skills for all children.	Allan Watson, 84 Uxbridge Road, London W13 8RA Tel: 020 8579 5108 www.nptrust.org.uk
National Society for the Prevention of Cruelty to Children (NSPCC)	Therapy and counselling for children and their families.	Weston House, 42 Curtain Road, London EC2A 3NH Helpline: 0808 800 5000 www.nspcc.org.uk
Office for Advice, Assistance, Support and Information on Special Needs (OAASIS)	An information service for parents and professionals about various learning disabilities.	Brock House, Grigg Lane, Brockenhurst. Hampshire SO42 7RE Helpline: 09068 633201 www.oaasis.co.uk
Online Asperger Syndrome Information and Support (OASIS)	An award-winning American website for parents and professionals.	www.udel.edu/bkirby/asperger
Organisation for Sickle Cell Anaemia Research (OSCAR)	Support for families.	5 Lauderdale House, Gosling Way, London SW9 6JS Tel: 020 7735 4166 www.oscartrust.cwc.net
Parents for Early Intervention in Autism in Children (PEACH)	Provides information and support for parents of children with autism.	The Brackens, London Road, Ascot, Berkshire SL5 8BE Tel: 01344 882248 www.peach.org.uk
Physically Handicapped and Able Bodied (PHAB)	Clubs, activities, outings and holidays.	Summit House, 50 Wandle Road, Croydon CR0 1DF Tel: 020 8667 9443 www.phabengland.org.uk
Prader-Willi Syndrome Association (PWSA UK)	Association for people and families affected by the syndrome, providing information and help.	125A London Road, Derby DE1 2QQ Tel: 01332 365676 www.pwsa-uk.demon.co.uk
Rathbone (formerly known as the **National Rathbone Society**)	A national charity which believes that progress is possible for all people. Advice, support and training for families and professionals in all aspects of SEN.	4th Floor, Churchgate House, 56 Oxford Street, Manchester M1 6EU Advice line: 0800 917 6790 www.rathci-ho.demon.co.uk
RNID (formerly the **Royal National Institute for Deaf People**)	Publications and educational advice regarding hearing impairment.	19–23 Featherstone Street, London EC1Y 8SL Helpline: 0808 808 0123 (Mon–Fri 9am–5pm) www.rnid.org.uk
Royal Association for Disability and Rehabilitation (RADAR)	Information and publications on disability.	12 City Forum, 250 City Road, London EC1V 8AF Tel: 020 7250 3222 www.radar.org.uk
Royal National Institute for the Blind (RNIB)	Information, publications and educational advice regarding visual impairment.	105 Judd Street, London WC1H 9NE Helpline: 0845 766 9999 (Mon–Fri 9am–5pm) www.rnib.org.uk
Sargent Cancer Care for Children	Support, information and counselling for young people up to the age of 21 and their families.	Griffin House, 161 Hammersmith Road, London W6 8SG Tel: 020 8752 2800 www.sargent.org

Organisation	Description	Contact details
Scope	Support, information and publications for children affected by cerebral palsy, and for their families.	6 Market Road, London N7 9PW Helpline: 0808 800 3333 www.scope.org.uk
Scottish Society for Autism	Support and information about autism.	Hilton House, Alloa Business Park, Whins Road, Alloa FK10 3SA Tel: 01259 720044 www.autism-in-scotland.org.uk
Sense (The National Deaf/Blind and Rubella Association)	Educational advice for parents of children with visual and hearing impairment – especially those damaged by rubella.	11–13 Clifton Terrace, Finsbury Park, London N4 3SR Tel: 020 7272 7774 www.sense.org.uk
Sickle Cell Society	Information and support.	54 Station Road, London NW10 4UA Tel: 020 8961 4006/7795 www.sicklecellsociety.org
Special Educational Needs Joint Initiative for Training (SENJIT)	Offers training, support and advice for staff involved in special needs. Services are based on a yearly subscription by the LEA. Includes 12 support groups.	Institute of Education, University of London. 20 Bedford Way, London WC1H 0AL www.ioe.ac.uk/teepnnp/SENJIT_Home.html
Speech and Language	A website run by two schools. Information for parents about speech and language disorders, including elective mutism. Also has useful guides to the special needs processes.	www.speechnlanguage.org.uk
Speech Teach	A website developed to provide links and teaching resources for parents and professionals supporting children with speech and learning difficulties.	www.speechteach.co.uk
Starlight Children's Foundation (UK)	A charity which aims to brighten the lives of seriously ill children.	Macmillan House, Paddington Station, London W2 1HD Tel: 020 7262 2881 www.starlight.org.uk
STEPS (The National Association for Children with Lower Limb Abnormalities)	A self-help group helping families of children with lower limb abnormalities.	Lymm Court, 11 Eagle Brow, Lymm, Cheshire WA13 0LP Helpline: 0871 717 0044 www.steps-charity.org.uk
Syndromes Without A Name (SWAN)	A website for parents whose children's conditions have not yet been diagnosed.	www.undiagnosed.clara.net
Tourette Syndrome Association (UK)	Provides information and coordinates support groups for families of children with the syndrome.	PO Box 26149, Dunfermline KY12 7YU Tel: 0845 458 1252 www.tsa.org.uk
Visual Impairment Centre for Teaching and Research (VICTAR)	Advice, resources and training.	School of Education, University of Birmingham, Edgbaston, Birmingham B15 2TT Tel: 0121 413 6733 www.education.bham.ac.uk/research/victar
WATCh (What About The Children?)	Charity which promotes parental responsibility, especially for children's emotional needs.	4 Upton Quarry, Langton Green, Kent TN3 0HA Tel: 01892 863245 www.jbaassoc.demon.co.uk/watch
Williams Syndrome Foundation	Information and support for parents.	161 High Street, Tonbridge, Kent, TN9 1BX Tel: 01732 365152 www.williams-syndrome.org.uk
Write Away for Friendship and Communication	Organises pen-friends for children with disabilities or special needs.	1 Thorpe Close, London W10 5XL Tel: 020 8964 4225 www.write-away.org
Young Minds	Charity committed to improving the mental health of all children and young people, providing information and support for parents, young people and professionals.	102–108 Clerkenwell Road, London EC1M 5SA Parents' helpline: 0800 018 2138 www.youngminds.org.uk

Special needs publishers

A–Z of publishers and groups who produce useful materials for supporting special needs children.

Although most of the following are commercial publishers, we have also included the names of voluntary support agencies who produce useful materials. These agencies are marked with an asterisk (*) and their contact details are given in full in the separate list of special needs support groups on pages 49–56 of this book. Many publishers have websites with online catalogues of their publications.

ACE Centre and Advisory Trust*

Has a range of publications about communication aids and services.

Addison Wesley Longman

Edinburgh Gate
Harlow
Essex CM20 2JE
Tel: 01279 623928
Publishes *Breakthrough to Literacy* sentence and word making materials.

AMS Educational

Woodside Trading Estate
Low Lane
Horsforth
Leeds LS18 5NY
Tel: 0113 258 0309
www.senter.co.uk
Supplies resources and suggests strategies for reluctant readers, particularly boys.

Ann Arbor Publishers Ltd

PO Box 1
Belford
Northumberland NE70 7JX
Tel: 01668 214460
www.annarbor.co.uk
Supplies a range of books, tracking materials, high interest novels with low reading levels and tests related to specific learning difficulties.

Association for all Speech Impaired Children (AFASIC)*

Produces a range of information sheets and other publications about speech and language impairment. It also publishes *Afasic Abstract* a twice-yearly journal about the latest research and issues related to language disorder.

Association for Spina Bifida and Hydrocephalus (ASBAH)*

Produces a bi-monthly magazine called *Link* as well as a range of pamphlets and information sheets on spina bifida and hydrocephalus.

AVP

School Hill Centre
Chepstow
Monmouthshire NP16 5PH
Tel: 01291 625439
www.avp.co.uk
Provides software and videos for all ages and abilities.

Mike Ayres Design and Development Ltd

The Paddocks
2 Ashfurlong Park
Door
Sheffield S17 3LD
Tel: 0114 235 6880
www.mike-ayres.co.uk
Suppliers of a range of children's play equipment.

Barrington Stoke

10 Belford Terrace
Edinburgh EH4 3DQ
Tel: 0131 315 4933
www.barringtonstoke.co.uk
Publishes books for reluctant readers particularly those with dyslexia. Children are encouraged to comment on story manuscripts before publication. Those children who make helpful comments receive a free copy of the book.

BEAM Education Ltd

Maze Workshops
72a Southgate Road
London N1 3JT
Tel: 020 7684 3323
www.beam.co.uk
Provides a range of stimulating resources for maths teaching across all abilities.

Belitha Press

64 Brewery Road
London N7 9NT
Tel: 020 7697 3000
www.chrysalisbooks.co.uk/childrens/
publishers/belitha
Produces books about disability for children.

Better Books

3 Paganel Drive
Dudley DY1 4AZ
Tel: 01384 253276
www.betterbooks.com
Supplies a wide range of books and learning materials particularly for people with specific learning difficulties.

Brilliant Publications

1 Church View
Sparrow Hall Farm
Edlesborough
Dunstable LU6 2ES
Tel: 01525 229720
www.brilliantpublications.co.uk
Produces books for older reluctant readers and young people with learning difficulties.

Buzan Centres Ltd

54 Parkstone Road
Poole
Dorset BH15 2PG.
Tel: 01202 674676
www.mind-map.com
Supplies books, videos and software about mind-mapping techniques.

Claire Publications (also Jonathan Press and Sweet Counter)
Unit 8 Tey Brook Craft Centre
Great Tey
Colchester CO6 1JE
Tel: 01206 211020
www.clairepublications.com
Produces a range of resources for primary and secondary children of all abilities, including gifted and talented children.

Crick Software
35 Charter Gate
Quarry Park Close
Northampton NN3 6QB
Tel: 01604 671691
www.cricksoft.co.uk
Reading and writing software for all ages and abilities. Winner of the Special Needs Software Award BETT 2002.

Crossbow Education
41 Sawpit Lane
Brocton
Stafford ST17 0TE
Tel: 01785 660920
www.crossboweducation.com
Provides games, photocopiable materials and practical resources for spelling, language and early maths skills for children with specific learning difficulties.

Drake Educational Associates
89 St Fagans Road
Fairwater
Cardiff CF5 3AE
Telephone: 029 2056 0333
www.drakeed.com
Specialises in multi-media resources for primary and middle schools. The main product is the *Language Master System* which helps develop language and literacy skills.

Dyscovery Centre*
Provides factsheets, videos, books and CD-Roms about a range of syndromes and disorders.

Dyslexia Institute*
Provides psychological assessment materials, resources and books for those working with children with specific learning difficulties.

Dyspraxia Foundation*
Provides books and factsheets related to dyspraxia.

Easylearn
Trent House
Fiskerton
Southwell NG25 0UH
Tel: 01636 830240
www.easylearn.co.uk
Provides photocopiable resources to support the literacy and numeracy hour – suitable for all ability ranges.

Educational Kinesiology Foundation (Edu-K)
12 Golders Rise
London NW4 2HR
Tel: 020 8202 3141
www.braingym.org.uk
Provides books, information and courses on brain gym.

Egon Publishers Ltd
15 Royston Road
Baldock
Hertfordshire SG7 6NW
Tel: 01462 894498
www.egon.co.uk
Provides a range of publications to support the learning of basic skills. Supplies *Spelling Made Easy* and *Maths Made Easy*.

First and Best in Education Ltd
Earlstrees Court
Earlstrees Road
Corby
Northamptonshire NN17 4HH
Tel: 01536 399005
www.firstandbest.co.uk
Publishes educational photocopiable books and e-books across a range of subjects and learning difficulties.

Formative Fun
Education House
Horn Park Business Centre
Broadwindsor Road
Beaminster DT8 3PT
Tel: 01308 868999
www.formative-fun.com
Provides a range of games and practical activities for primary children of all abilities, particularly early years. Has a number of shops around the UK.

David Fulton Publishers
The Chiswick Centre
414 Chiswick High Road
London W4 5TF
Tel: 020 8996 3610
www.fultonpublishers.co.uk

Provides a wide range of books giving advice on teaching children with special needs.

Galt Educational and Pre-School
Johnsonbrook Road
Hyde
Cheshire SK14 4QT
Tel: 08451 203005
www.galt-educational.co.uk
Provides a wide range of educational products including toys, games, role-play equipment and classroom furniture.

Harcourt Brace
See The Psychological Corporation.

HELP Educational Games
PO Box 412
Amersham
Buckinghamshire HP7 9WB
Tel: 01494 765261
www.helpgames.co.uk
Supplies a wide range of reading and spelling games.

Hope Education
Hyde Buildings, Ashton Road
Hyde
Cheshire SK14 4SH
Tel: 0845 120 2055
www.hope-education.co.uk
Supplies a wide variety of educational products suitable for Key Stages 1 and 2.

Hopscotch Educational Publishing Ltd
29 Waterloo Place
Leamington Spa
Warwickshire CV32 5LA
Tel: 01926 744227
www.hopscotchbooks.com
Provides a range of books to support the development of basic literacy and numeracy skills in the primary school. It also provides books that support the development of literacy skills across other areas of the curriculum.

Hornsby International Dyslexia Centre
Wye Street
London SW11 2HB
Tel: 020 7223 1144
www.hornsby.co.uk
The centre has a lending library and bookshop with books, workbooks, games and software to support specific learning difficulties.

iANSYST Ltd
Fen House
Fen Road
Cambridge CB4 1UN
Tel: 01223 420101
www.iansyst.co.uk
Provides a wide range of software, gadgets and other products for those with dyslexia, visual impairments and other disabilities.

Inclusive Technology Ltd
Gatehead Business Park
Delph New Road
Delph
Oldham OL3 5BX
Tel: 01457 819790
www.inclusive.co.uk
Provides technology and software to support inclusion.

Don Johnston Special Needs
18 Clarendon Court
Calver Road
Winwick Quay
Warrington WA2 8QP
Tel: 01925 241642
www.donjohnston.com/uk
Supplier of hardware and software products for special needs.

Jolly Learning Ltd
Tailours House
High Road
Chigwell
Essex IG7 6DL
Tel: 020 8501 0405
www.jollylearning.co.uk
Publisher of *Jolly Phonics* and *Jolly Grammar*.

Kick Start Publications
38 Awebridge Road
Netherton
Dudley
West Midlands DY2 0JA
Tel: 01384 258535
www.specialbooks.net
Provides a range of materials covering phonics, reading, spelling and number skills designed for children with specific learning difficulties.

Hilda King Educational
Ashwells Manor Drive
Penn
Buckinghamshire HP10 8EU
Tel: 01494 813947
www.hildaking.co.uk

Publishes a wide range of photocopiable resources for both mainstream and special needs to support the development of basic literacy skills.

Jessica Kingsley Publishers
116 Pentonville Road
London N1 9JB
Tel: 020 7833 2307
www.jkp.com
Publishes textbooks and reference books on social work, disabilities, art therapies and education.

LDA
Duke Street
Wisbech
Cambridgeshire PE13 2AE
Tel: 01945 463441
www.ldalearning.com
Supplies a wide range of products for children at every stage of development, including special needs (separate catalogues are available for different curriculum areas).

Learn How Publications
10 Townsend Avenue
Southgate
London N14 7HJ
Tel: 020 8542 4642
www.learnhowpublications.co.uk
Produces *IEP Writer* software, which can create individual plans for special needs education in nursery, primary and secondary schools.

Learning Materials Ltd
Dixon Street
Wolverhampton WV2 2BX
Telephone: 01902 454026
www.learning.material.btinternet.co.uk
Produces photocopiable resource material, audio cassettes and CD-Roms for children with special needs. The materials support learning across the curriculum.

Lucky Duck Publishing
3 Thorndale Mews
Clifton
Bristol BS8 2HX
Tel: 0117 973 2881
www.luckyduck.co.uk
Publishes videos, books and training materials focusing on a variety of special needs issues.

National Association for Special Educational Needs (NASEN)*
Produces a range of useful guides and handbooks for teachers of children with SEN.

NES Arnold Ltd
Findel House, Excelsior Road
Ashby Park
Ashby de la Zouch
Leicestershire LE65 1NG
Tel: 0845 120 4525
enquiries@nesarnold.co.uk
www.nesarnold.co.uk
Supplies practical educational products to support teaching across the curriculum (including *Multilink*, *Clixi* and *Kiblo* construction sets).

nferNelson Publishing Co Ltd
Unit 28 Bramble Road
Techno Trading Centre
Swindon
Wiltshire SN2 8EZ
Tel: 0845 602 1937
www.nfer-nelson.co.uk
Provides specialist assessments and resources for children and young people from birth to 19, for use by speech and language therapists, educational psychologists, SEN coordinators and specialist teachers.

pfp publishing ltd
FREEPOST LON20579
London WC1X 8BR
Tel: 0845 602 4337
www.pfp-publishing.com
Publishers of essential management information for special needs coordinators and teacher resources.

Philip and Tacey Ltd
North Way
Andover
Hampshire SP10 5BA
Tel: 01264 332171
www.philipandtacey.co.uk
Supplies a wide range of educational products for children at every stage of development, including special needs supporting most areas of the curriculum.

Prim-Ed Publishing
4th Floor Tower Court
Foleshill Enterprise Park
Courtaulds Way
Coventry CV6 5NX
Tel: 0870 876 0151
www.prim-ed.com

Publishes photocopiable resources for primary and lower secondary school special needs children. Nearly all the pages of every book can be viewed online.

The Psychological Corporation
Harcourt Education
Hally Court
Jordan Hill
Oxford OX2 8EJ
Tel: 01865 888188
www.tpc-international.com
Provides a range of assessment and intervention materials for teachers and other professionals working with children with special needs.

The Questions Publishing Company Ltd
Leonard House
321 Bradford Street
Digbeth
Birmingham B5 6ET
Tel: 0121 666 7878
www.education-quest.com
Publishes a range of magazines including *Special Children*. Subscribers have access to educational archive material online.

Royal Association for Disability and Rehabilitation (RADAR)*
Publications for teachers and parents of children with disabilities.

R-E-M
Great Western House
Langport
Somerset TA10 9YU
Tel: 01458 254700
www.r-e-m.co.uk
Provides software and hardware to aid inclusion for all ages.

Rompa
Goyt Side Road
Chesterfield
Derbyshire S40 2PH
Tel: 01246 211777
www.rompa.com
Supplies products to improve the quality of life for those with movement and sensory difficulties. Many are suitable for children with motor coordination difficulties.

Select Educational Equipment
Unit 4 Arcadia Park
Towers Business Park
Wheelhouse Road
Rugeley WS15 1UZ
Tel: 01889 578333

Provides a range of products to support the development of skills across the curriculum.

SEMERC
Granada Learning
Quay Street
Manchester M60 9EX
Tel: 0161 827 2719
www.semerc.com
Provides access devices, software, hardware and training for special needs ICT support.

Speechmark Publishing (formerly known as **Winslow Press Ltd**)
Telford Road
Bicester
Oxfordshire OX26 4LQ
Telephone: 01869 244644
www.winslow-press.co.uk
Provides a wide range of practical resources for children and adults who have special needs. Also produces books and videos for professionals working with people who have learning difficulties as well as a wide range of practical activities designed to support the development of specific skills.

Supportive Learning Publications
23 West View
Chirk
Wrexham LL14 5HL
Tel: 01691 774778
www.slp.demon.co.uk
Provides resources for Key Stages 1 and 2 as well as for pupils with learning difficulties.

Taskmaster Ltd
Morris Road
Leicester LE2 6BR
Tel: 0116 270 4286
www.taskmasteronline.co.uk
Provides teaching aids, resources and support materials for maths, special needs and speech and language difficulties.

Thrass (UK) Limited
Units 1–3 Tarvin Sands
Barrow Lane
Tarvin
Chester CH3 8JF
Tel: 01829 741413
www.thrass.co.uk
Produces resources that support the teaching of reading and spelling, using the 44 phonemes (speech sounds) of spoken English and the

graphemes (spelling choices) of written English.

Tumble Tots Equipment
Blue Bird Park
Bromsgrove Road
Hunnington
Halesowen
West Midlands B62 0TT
Tel: 0121 585 7003
www.tumbletots.com
Provides coordination equipment, books, puzzles, soft toys, videos, CD-Roms and audio cassettes to support early development.

Wesco
114 Highfields Road
Witham
Essex CM8 2HH
Tel: 01376 503590
www.wesco-group.com
Supplies a large selection of teaching equipment and products to encourage learning from birth to age six. Products support most early learning skills' development.

Whurr Publications Ltd
19b Compton Terrace
London N1 2UN
Tel: 020 7359 5979
www.whurr.co.uk
Publishes books and journals on special needs, nursing, therapy, physiotherapy, audiology, psychology and psychiatry for professionals. Specialises in books on dyslexia for teachers and parents.

Widgit Software
124 Cambridge Science Park
Milton Road
Cambridge CB4 0ZS
Tel: 01223 425558
www.widgit.co.uk
Provides software to support special needs and has developed *Writing with Symbols*.

Winslow Press Ltd (Education and Special Needs)
See Speechmark Publishing.

Special needs jargon-buster

A–Z glossary of the most common special needs jargon.

As a special needs coordinator or a teacher of a child with special needs you will encounter a great deal of professional jargon in your job. This glossary will help you to sift your way through it all and, equally importantly, to explain special needs terms to non-experts such as parents, other teachers and teaching assistants.

Annual review – a meeting held annually to review the statement of special educational need. If a statement has been issued, this will be looked at closely by all the professionals involved. The child's parents, and often the child, will be invited to attend. Everyone discusses how the child is progressing and agrees any changes that may be needed in the support that is being given (called provision). Everyone agrees whether to continue with the current provision, request more provision, suggest different provision, reduce the provision or cease maintaining the statement.

Articulation – the way that speech sounds are made from movements of the lips, jaw and tongue.

Association – the ability to relate concepts presented through the senses (visual, auditory and kinaesthetic).

Attention span – the amount of time children can concentrate on a task without being distracted or losing interest.

Auditory discrimination – the ability to listen to sounds and detect similarities and differences between them. This could involve being able to discriminate between larger sounds made by animals, vehicles, etc., or being able to detect similarities and differences between sounds in words.

Auditory figure-ground discrimination – the ability to focus on a specific sound, despite background noise.

Auditory learning style – children who are auditory learners do best when they are involved in speaking and listening tasks.

Auditory memory – the ability to recall information that has been given orally. The information may be retained for a short while (short-term memory), rehearsed and retained for a longer period of time (long-term memory) or retained and recalled in the correct sequence (auditory sequential memory).

Auditory sequential memory – the ability to recall sounds, spoken words and information in the sequence in which they were heard.

Auditory synthesis – the ability to blend sounds into syllables and syllables into words.

Baseline assessment – the assessment of infant children's basic skills on school entry or during the Reception year in school. It is undertaken by teachers and provides a baseline from which subsequent performance can be monitored.

Behaviour modification – a technique that aims to change behaviour patterns by giving rewards for positive behaviour and deliberately seeming not to notice negative behaviour.

Behaviour support plan – the action plan implemented by an LEA to deal with behaviour problems.

Centile – a term used in a number of tests that measures children's ability against a national standard. If a child is at the fiftieth centile in a particular test, that means that he has scored the average level in that test. 50 per cent of the general school population at that age would score higher. Similarly, the first centile means that the child has scored in the first one per cent of the population, with 99 per cent of children scoring higher than that.

Child Protection Register – the central register (kept by social services) of children in the area who are considered to be suffering, or to be likely to suffer, significant harm and who are the subject of a child protection plan.

Children in need – those children who may not achieve or maintain a reasonable standard of health or development without extra help. It can also describe a child whose health may suffer without additional provision or who is disabled.

Code of Practice – the document, published by the government in 2001, setting out the statutory duties of LEAs, schools, early education settings and health and social services. It provides a framework for the identification and assessment of children with special needs. It also provides guidelines for making effective provision for these children. Parents can ask to see a copy of the Code of Practice in school. This SEN Code of Practice should not be confused with the Disability Discrimination Act Code of Practice for Schools, published in 2002, which is also of relevance to SEN coordinators and school management.

Cognition – the process of knowing, thinking and reasoning.

Cognitive ability – the intellectual ability to know, think and reason.

Congenital – refers to a condition (such as congenital heart disease) which is found to be in existence at or before birth. The word congenital does not necessarily mean that the condition is hereditary.

Coordination – the ability to perform complex body movements through the harmonious functioning of the muscles in the body.

Cross dominance – also called mixed dominance. It is when a person's preferred or leading eye, hand, and foot are not all on the same side of the body. For example, a person may be right-footed and right-eyed but left-handed.

Decoding – the process of extracting meaning from written or spoken symbols.

Developmental delay – a term used to describe children who have not mastered the skills expected for their age. Developmental delays can be across a range of areas – social, emotional, physical, intellectual and self-help skills. The term can also be used when describing difficulties experienced by children with severe sensory, congenital or mental conditions.

Directionality – the ability to know and interpret direction and orientation eg. right/left, up/down, forward/backward.

Disapplication – when a child is considered unable to study the National Curriculum for a short period of time, or when a child is not included in the end of Key Stage 1 or Key Stage 2 tests. The parents, school and local education authority should all be involved in agreeing whether this is to happen. Disapplication can be applied to children with or without a statement of special educational need.

Discrimination – the ability to detect similarities and differences between stimuli.

Distractability – the inability to attend to a task without being distracted by other sights, sounds and movements within the environment.

Early Learning Goals – it is expected that most children will reach these levels, in six areas, by the end of the Foundation Stage.

Early Years Action – when provision is made for a child by the special needs coordinator and teacher in the early years setting that is additional to or different from what is normally provided. The child will be identified as having special educational needs and will usually have an IEP.

Early Years Action Plus – when specialist advice and support for a child has been given to the special needs coordinator and teacher in the early years setting so that provision can be made that is additional to or different from what is normally provided. The child will be identified as having special educational needs and will have an IEP reflecting the specialist advice.

Encoding – the ability to formulate ideas and then to select sounds and words with which to express them through speaking or writing.

Expressive language – the ability to communicate, expressing thoughts and responses through writing, speaking or signs and gestures.

Eye-hand coordination – the ability of the eyes and hands to work together to complete a task as in drawing and writing.

Figure-ground discrimination – the ability to distinguish important information from the surrounding environment despite background noises and visual distractions.

Fine motor – refers to the ability to use the smaller muscles in the body for precise tasks such as writing, drawing, sewing, using scissors or tying shoe laces.

Foundation Stage – pre-school and Reception children aged between 3 and 5 years.

Graduated approach – this approach recognises that there is a 'continuum of special educational needs' and that specialist action and intervention should be based on the degree (or severity when seen on a spectrum) of special needs of the child and the difficulties they are experiencing.

Gross motor – refers to the ability to use the larger muscles in the body for activities that require strength, coordination and balance, such as climbing, walking, running and jumping.

Group education plan – when a group of children have similar learning difficulties then group targets can be set instead of separate IEPs.

Home-school agreement – the written contract that is drawn up between the school, parents or carers and the child. It sets out expectations of attendance, behaviour, standards of education and homework.

Hyperactivity – the inability to focus on one task for a period of time and the need to be constantly on the move.

Hypoactivity – the opposite of hyperactivity. Children who are hypoactive, though also unable to concentrate, often appear to be in a daze and to lack energy.

Impulsivity – when children react to a situation without considering the consequences.

Inclusion – the word used to denote that children with special needs and other differences are included in a mainstream school. Inclusion enables children with special needs to be involved in activities with children who don't have special needs, which often has benefits for both.

Individual education plan (IEP) – the plan devised for meeting a child's needs. It is prepared specially for the child concerned. It sets out what will be done in the following weeks to support the child, who will do it and what resources will be required. It also sets out specific targets for the child. IEPs are usually reviewed by the school every term or half-term, or more often if required. Parents (and children if possible) are invited to discuss and review the plan and to help decide on new targets.

Insertions – when children add letters or numbers to words or numerals that should not be there eg. reading an additional word in a sentence, which is not printed on the page.

Integration – the process whereby children return to mainstream education after spending part of their education in a special unit or school or having home tuition.

Inversions – when children confuse the up/down directionality of letters or numbers eg. b/p, 6/9.

IQ – acronym for intelligence quotient. It is the ratio between a person's chronological age (measured in years) and mental (cognitive) age, as measured by a standardised intelligence test, multiplied by 100.

Key Stage 1 (KS1) – children aged 5–7 (formerly known as infants).

Key Stage 2 (KS2) – children aged 7–11 (formerly known as juniors).

Kinaesthetic learning style – children who are kinaesthetic learners do best when they are actively involved in practical tasks which rely on the use of movement and touch.

Laterality – the tendency to use the (dominant) hand, foot, eye, and ear on a particular side of the body. Many people use their right hand when writing and their right foot when kicking.

LEA – acronym for local education authority, which is the local government body responsible for some aspects of education in a local area.

Learning difficulties – refers to the specific problems a child may have with any aspects of the learning process.

Mixed laterality – the tendency to use either (both) right or left sides of the body for different tasks.

Modification – the National Curriculum can be changed or modified to help a child with special educational needs to follow the learning in an area of the curriculum.

Multisensory – refers to a method of learning or a range of activities which involve using most or all of the senses.

Note in lieu – a note that is sent to the parents when an LEA decides not to issue a statement of special educational need. The note in lieu should describe the child's special needs, explain the reasons why the LEA is not issuing a statement and should contain recommendations for suitable provision for the child. The note may be sent to the school with the parent's permission. This is not a legally binding document.

Opportunity playgroups – pre-school settings which provide play activities and therapy for young children with special educational needs. They can take children from a very young age.

Perceptual ability – the function of the brain to process, interpret and organise information received through the senses.

Placement – the school or unit in which a child with special needs is placed after careful consideration has been given to their specific needs.

Portage – an educational home visiting service for pre-school children whose development is significantly delayed. It is named after the town in the US where the scheme originated. A portage supervisor, who is usually an educational psychologist, visits the home to assess the child and answer any questions. Then a trained home visitor teaches parents or carers activities to help stimulate the child's development.

P scales – very small steps of progression across the curriculum by which the progress of special needs children can be measured.

Proposed statement – the draft statement that is sent to the parents by the LEA, setting out the proposed arrangements for the education of their child. Parents have 15 days from the receipt of the proposed statement to make any comments.

Receptive language – the ability to receive and comprehend verbal language, either written or spoken.

Reversals – reversal is a perceptual difficulty resulting in letters, words and numbers being reversed eg. b/d, was/saw, 12/21.

School Action – when provision is made for a child by the special needs coordinator and class teacher that is additional to or different from what is normally provided within a differentiated setting. The child will have been identified as having special educational needs and will usually have an IEP.

School Action Plus – when specialist advice and support for a child has been given to the special needs coordinator and teacher so that provision can be made that is additional to or different from what is normally provided within a differentiated setting. The child will have been identified as having special educational needs and will have an IEP reflecting the specialist advice.

Self-esteem – how positively (high self-esteem) or negatively (low self-esteem) children perceive themselves within their environment.

Semantic knowledge – the ability to understand the meaning of words in different contexts and the knowledge of the meanings of relationships between words eg. categories, opposites, synonyms, association. It also includes an ability to understand narrative.

SEN register – the system which records when a concern was first raised, the kind of support that is being given, dates of IEP reviews and details of children who have moved off the SEN support list. Figures (but no names) from the register may be used by the school governors, LEA or government agencies.

Sensory-motor – refers to the relationship between sensation and movement.

Sequence – information arranged in a particular order eg. days of the week, months of the year.

Sight words – words that children can recognise as whole words on sight.

Sight word approach – a method of teaching reading which relies heavily upon a child's visual memory skills, used for recognising whole words, rather than on phoneme blending.

Sound blending – the ability to blend the component phonemes into whole words.

Spatial awareness – the ability to be aware of oneself in one's space in terms of position, distance, form and direction.

Spatial relationships – how different objects relate to one another and to the child himself.

Special school – a school that is specially organised to support children with a statement of special educational need. There are often specialist teachers and resources on site and children are taught in smaller groups.

Statement of special educational need – the document issued by the LEA which contains details of the child's educational needs, as identified by the local authority during the statutory assessment. It includes details of the provision required to meet those needs. The statement names the school that the child will attend (agreed with the parents and the school). Usually, this will be the school the child already attends, but occasionally a special school is considered to be more suitable. The statement will not include anything that parents have not already discussed or been made aware of.

Statutory assessment – the process which takes place if the LEA believes that it needs to outline the child's needs, at the request of the school, parent or another agency. It does not always lead to a statement of special educational need. The authority looks at all that has been done for the child, reports from professionals and previous IEPs. An educational psychologist assesses the child and prepares a report. The SEN section of the local authority considers all the evidence and makes a decision as to whether to give a statement.

Substitution – when letters, numbers or words are interchanged when reading, spelling or in numeracy eg. 'wos' for 'was' in spelling, or 'sad' for 'said' in reading.

Syntax – the grammar of spoken language and written sentences, involving how words are sequenced to convey meaning.

Syndrome – a set of symptoms that indicates a specific disorder.

Tactile – relating to the sense of touch.

Thinking skills – the skills through which children acquire, interpret, reorganise, store, retrieve, and synthesise knowledge.

Transposition – when the order of letters in a word or digits in a number is confused eg. gril/girl, 546/654.

Tribunal – an independent body that hears appeals by parents against LEA decisions on assessments and statements. For example, parents may appeal to this body if a request for a statement has been turned down. The decision of the tribunal is final. This tribunal is now called the SENDisT (SEN and Disability Tribunal).

VAK – acronym for visual, auditory, kinaesthetic which relates to the way that we give and receive information. We each have a preferred learning style, either visual, auditory or kinaesthetic, and if we are given opportunities to learn using this style we tend to learn in a more natural and more effective way.

Verbal comprehension – the ability to listen to information, remember it, understand it and then use the information across a range of tasks.

Visual association – the ability to relate concepts which are presented visually through words or pictures.

Visual discrimination – the ability to detect similarities or differences between materials which are presented visually.

Visual learning style – children who are visual learners do best when they are involved in tasks using written language and visual materials.

Visual memory – the ability to recall information that has been presented visually. The information may be retained for a short while (short-term memory), rehearsed and retained for a longer period of time (long-term memory) or retained and recalled in the correct sequence (visual sequential memory).

Visual-motor – refers to the ability to translate information received visually into a motor response. Children who have difficulties in this area often have poor handwriting.

Visual perception – the ability to recognise, interpret and organise visual images.

Word attack skills – the ability to analyse unfamiliar words both visually and phonetically.

Word recognition – the ability to read or pronounce a word but does not necessarily imply understanding of the meaning of the word.